RAPID MATH

"Let us watch well our beginnings and results will manage themselves."

ALEXANDER CLARK

RAPID MATH

SHORTCUTS TO MASTERING
Rapid Addition
Rapid Subtraction

QUICK METHODS FOR
Division
Multiplication
Fractions

A. FREDERICK COLLINS

BARNES & NOBLE
BOOKS
NEW YORK

This edition published by Barnes & Noble, Inc.,
by arrangement with Carol Publishing Group.

1998 Barnes & Noble Books

ISBN 0-7607-0912-2

Printed and bound in the United States of America

98 99 00 01 02 M 9 8 7 6 5 4 3 2 1

FG

INTRODUCTION

A. Frederick Collins was both a physicist and mathematician of note. One of his major contributions, *The Amateur Radio Handbook,* has recently been revised for the publication of a 15th edition.

In this book Collins stresses the importance of being able to do mathematical calculations in one's head, rapidly and correctly. While "figuring" is the basis of all business, it is not restricted to business alone. Today, every housewife, every farmer, every student has to be able to manipulate numbers correctly in order to manage his or her affairs.

As business grows increasingly complex (every middle-sized and small enterprise must have a small computer, and the big ones cannot manage without sophisticated electronic equipment), so are the mathematical affairs of each individual becoming increasingly complicated.

The housewife must be able to add and multiply quickly in her head while in the supermarket in order to ascertain the relative values of different cuts of meats, the sizes and contents of various canned goods, and whether or not she is being overcharged.

The farmer must be adept in calculating the mixing of feeds, the contents of silos, etc.

The importer must be able to calculate duties quickly; the storekeeper must be able to handle chain discounts; the taxi driver has to worry about income taxes, miles per gallon, etc.

Some sage once stated that there is no royal road to knowledge. This is *not* applicable to the book you now hold in your hand.

With proper *minimum* application to the information herein contained, you will rapidly attain maximum proficiency in the manipulation of numbers in your own daily life.

This is a book of mathematical shortcuts.

Take advantage of it.

THE PUBLISHERS

RAPID MATH

CONTENTS

CHAPTER		PAGE
I.	WHAT ARITHMETIC IS	1
II.	RAPID ADDITION	16
III.	RAPID SUBTRACTION	28
IV.	SHORT CUTS IN MULTIPLICATION	35
V.	SHORT CUTS IN DIVISION	56
VI.	SHORT CUTS IN FRACTIONS	64
VII.	EXTRACTING SQUARE AND CUBE ROOTS	74
VIII.	USEFUL TABLES AND FORMULAS	80
IX.	MAGIC WITH FIGURES	98

CHAPTER I

WHAT ARITHMETIC IS.

The Origin of Calculation.
The Origin of Counting and Figures.
Other Signs Used in Arithmetic.
The Four Ground Rules.
The Operation of Addition.
The Operation of Multiplication.
The Operation of Division.
The Operation of Subtraction.
Fractions.
Decimals.
Powers and Roots.
Ratios and Proportions.
Practical Applications of Arithmetic.
Percentage.
Interest.
Simple Interest.
Compound Interest.
Profit and Loss.
Gross Profit.
Net Profit.
Loss.
Reduction of Weights and Measures.

The Origin of Calculation. — To be able to figure in the easiest way and in the shortest time you should have a clear idea of what arithmetic is and of the ordinary methods used in calculation.

To begin with arithmetic means that we take certain numbers we already know about, that is the *value* of, and by manipulating them, that is performing an operation with them, we are able to find some number which we do not know but which we want to know.

Now our ideas about numbers are based entirely on our ability to measure things and this in turn is founded on the needs of our daily lives.

To make these statements clear suppose that *distance* did not concern us and that it would not take a longer *time* or greater *effort* to walk a mile than it would to walk a block. If such a state of affairs had always existed then primitive man never would have needed to judge that a day's walk was once again as far as half a day's walk.

In his simple reckonings he performed not only *the operation of addition* but he also laid the foundation for the measurement of *time.*

Likewise when primitive man considered the difference in the length of two paths which led, let us say, from his cave to the pool where the mastodons came to drink, and he gauged them so that he could choose the shortest way, he performed the operation of *subtraction* though he did not work it out arithmetically, for figures had yet to be invented.

And so it was with his food. The scarcity of it made the Stone Age man lay in a supply to tide over his wants until he could replenish his stock; and if he had a family he meted out an equal portion of each delicacy to each member, and in this way the fractional measurement of things came about.

There are three general divisions of measurements and these are (1) the measurement of *time;* (2) the measurement of *space* and (3) the measurement of *matter;* and on these three fundamental elements of nature through which all phenomena are manifested to us arithmetical operations of every kind are based if the calculations are of any practical use.[1]

The Origin of Counting and Figures. — As civilization grew on apace it was not enough for man to measure things by comparing them roughly with other things which formed his units, by the sense of sight or the physical efforts involved, in order to accomplish a certain result, as did his savage forefathers.

And so *counting*, or *enumeration* as it is called, was invented, and since man had five digits[2] on each hand it was the most natural thing in the world that he should have learned to count on his digits, and children still very often use their digits for this purpose and occasionally grown-ups too.

Having made each digit a unit, or *integer* as it is called, the next step was to give each one a definite name to call the unit by, and then came the writing of each one, not in unwieldy words

[1] To measure *time*, *space*, and *matter*, or as these elements are called in physics *time*, *length*, and *mass*, each must have a unit of its own so that other quantities of a like kind can be compared with them. Thus the unit of time is the *second;* the unit of length is the *foot*, and the unit of mass is the pound, hence these form what is called the *foot-pound-second* system. All other units relating to motion and force may be easily obtained from the F.P.S. system.

[2] The word *digit* means any one of the terminal members of the hand including the thumb, whereas the word *finger* excludes the thumb. Each of the Arabic numerals, 1, 2, 3, 4, 5, 6, 7, 8, 9, 0, is called a *digit* and is so named in virtue of the fact that the fingers were first used to count upon.

but by a simple mark, or a combination of marks called a *sign* or *symbol*, and which as it has come down to us is 1, 2, 3, 4, 5, 6, 7, 8, 9, 0.

By the time man had progressed far enough to name and write the symbols for the units he had two of the four *ground rules*, or *fundamental operations* as they are called, well in mind, as well as the combination of two or more figures to form numbers as 10, 23, 108, etc.

Other Signs Used in Arithmetic. — Besides the symbols used to denote the figures there are symbols employed to show what arithmetical operation is to be performed.

$+$ Called *plus*. It is the sign of *addition;* that is, it shows that two or more figures or numbers are to be added to make more, or to find the sum of them, as $5 + 10$. The plus sign was invented by Michael Stipel in 1544 and was used by him in his *Arithmetica Integra*.

$=$ Called *equal*. It is the sign of *equality* and it shows that the numbers on each side of it are of the same amount or are of *equal value*, as $5 + 10 = 15$. The sign of equality was published for the first time by Robert Recorde in 1557, who used it in his algebra.

$-$ Called *minus*. It is the sign of *subtraction* and it shows that a number is to be taken away or *subtracted* from another given number, as $10 - 5$. The minus sign was also invented by Michael Stipel.

× Called *times.* It is the sign of *multiplication* and means *multiplied by;* that is, taking one number as many times as there are units in the other, thus, 5 × 10. The sign of multiplication was devised by William Oughtred in 1631. It was called St. Andrew's Cross and was first published in a work called *Clavis Mathematicae,* or Key to Mathematics.

÷ Called the *division sign.* It is the sign of division and means *divided by;* that is, it shows a given number is to be contained in, or divided by, another given number, as 10 ÷ 5. The division sign was originated by Dr. John Pell, a professor of mathematics and philosophy.

The Four Ground Rules. — In arithmetic the operations of addition, subtraction, multiplication, and division are called the *ground rules* because all other operations such as fractions, extracting roots, etc., are worked out by them.

The Operation of Addition. — The ordinary definition of addition is the operation of finding a number which is equal to the value of two or more numbers.

This means that in addition we start with an unknown quantity which is made up of two or more known parts and by operating on these parts in a certain way we are able to find out exactly what the whole number of parts, or the unknown quantity, is.

To simply count up the numbers of parts is not

enough to perform the operation of addition, for when this is done we still have an unknown quantity. But to actually find what the *whole* number of parts is, or the *sum* of them as it is called, we have to count off all of the units of all of the numbers, thus:

$$2 + 2 + 2 + 2 = 8$$

Now when arithmetic began prehistoric man had to add these parts by using his fingers and saying 1 and 1 are 2, and 1 are 3, and 1 are 4, and so on, adding up each unit until he got the desired result.

Some time after, and it was probably a good many thousands of years, an improvement was made in figuring and the operation was shortened so that it was only necessary to say 2 + 2 are 4, and 2 are 6, and 2 are 8. When man was able to add four 2's without having to count each unit in each number he had made wonderful progress and it could not have taken him long to learn to add up other figures in the same way.

The Operation of Subtraction. — Subtraction is the operation of taking one number from the other and finding the difference between them.

To define subtraction in another and more simple way, we can say that it is the operation of starting with a known quantity which is made up of two or more parts and by taking a given number of parts from it we can find what the difference or remainder is in known parts. Hence the operation of subtraction is just the inverse of that of addition.

The processes of the mind which lead up to the operation of subtraction are these: when man began to concern himself with figures and he wanted to take 4 away from 8 and to still know how many remained he had to count the units that were left thus:

$$1 + 1 + 1 + 1 = 4$$

And finally, when he was able through a better understanding of figures and with a deal of practice to say $8 - 4 = 4$, without having to work it all out in units, he had made a great stride and laid down the second ground rule of arithmetic. But, curiously enough, the best method in use at the present time for performing the operation of subtraction is by addition, which is a reversion to first principles, as we shall presently see in Chapter III.

The Operation of Multiplication. — The rule for *multiplication* states that it is the operation of taking one number as many times as there are units in another.

In the beginning of arithmetic, when one number was to be taken as many times as there were units in another, the *product* was obtained by cumulative addition, the figures being added together thus:

$$7 + 7 + 7 + 7 + 7 = 35$$

Having once found that 7 taken 5 times gave the product 35 it was a far easier mental process to remember the fact, namely, that

$$7 \times 5 = 35$$

than it was to add up the five 7's each time; that is if the operation had to be done very often, and so another great short cut was made in the operation of addition and mental calculation took another step forward.

But multiplication was not only a mere matter of memorizing the fact that $7 \times 5 = 35$ but it meant that at least 100 other like operations had to be remembered and this resulted in the invention of that very useful arithmetical aid — the *multiplication table.*

While multiplication is a decided short cut in solving certain problems in addition, it is a great deal more than addition for it makes use of the relation, or *ratio* as it is called, between two numbers or two quantities of the same kind and this enables complex problems to be performed in an easy and rapid manner.

Hence the necessity for the absolute mastery of the multiplication table, as this is the master-key which unlocks many of the hardest arithmetical problems.

A quick memory and the multiplication table well learned will bring about a result so that the product of any two factors will be on the tip of your tongue or at the point of your pencil, and this will insure a rapidity of calculation that cannot be had in any other way.

The Operation of Division. — Division is the operation of finding one of two numbers called the *factors*, that is, the *divisor* and the *quotient*, when the whole number, or *dividend* as it is called, and the factor called the divisor are known.

Defined in more simple terms, division is the operation of finding how many times one number is contained in another number. Hence division, it will be seen, is simply the inverse operation of multiplication.

Since division and multiplication are so closely related it would seem that division should not have been very hard to learn in the beginning but *long division* was, nevertheless, an operation that could only be done by an expert arithmetician.

It will make division an easier operation if it is kept in mind that it is the inverse of multiplication; that is, the operation of division annuls the operation of multiplication, since if we multiply 4 by 3 we get 12 and if we divide 12 by 3 we get 4, and we are back to the place we started from. For this reason problems in division can be proved by multiplication and conversely multiplication can be proved by division.

Fractions. — A fraction is any part of a whole number or unit. While a whole number may be divided into any number of fractional parts the fractions are in themselves numbers just the same. Without fractions there could be no measurement and the more numerous the fractional divisions of a thing the more accurately it can be measured.

From the moment that man began to measure off distances and quantities he began to use fractions, and so if fractions were not used before whole numbers they were certainly used concurrently with them. In fact the idea of a whole number is made clearer to the mind by thinking of a number of parts as making up the whole than by considering the whole as a unit in itself.

It will be seen then that while fractions are parts of whole numbers they are in themselves numbers and as such they are subject to the same treatment as whole numbers; that is operations based on the four ground rules, namely, addition, subtraction, multiplication, and division.

Fractions may be divided into two general classes and these are (1) *common* or *vulgar* [1] *fractions* and (2) *decimal fractions.* Vulgar fractions may be further divided into (A) *proper fractions* and (B) *improper fractions*, and both vulgar and decimal fractions may be operated as (a) *simple fractions*, (b) *compound fractions*, and (c) *complex fractions*, the latter including *continued fractions*, all of which is explained in Chapter VI.

[1] Once upon a time anything that was common or ordinary was called *vulgar*, hence common fractions were and are still called vulgar fractions.

Decimals. — Since there are five digits on each hand it is easy to see how the *decimal system*, in which numbers are grouped into tens, had its origin.

The word *decimal* means 10 and decimal arithmetic is based on the number 10; that is, all operations use powers of 10 or of $\frac{1}{10}$. But instead of writing the terms down in vulgar fractions as $\frac{1}{10}$, $\frac{5}{10}$, or $\frac{5}{100}$, these terms are expressed as whole numbers thus .1, .5, .05 when the fractional value is made known by the position of the *decimal point*.

This being true the four fundamental operations may be proceeded with just as though whole numbers were being used and this, of course, greatly simplifies all calculations where fractions are factors, that is, provided the decimal system can be used at all.

It is not often, though, except in calculations involving money or where the *metric system* [1] of weights and measures is used, that the decimal system can be applied with exactness, for few common fractions can be stated exactly by them; that is, few common fractions can be changed to decimal fractions and not leave a remainder.

Powers and Roots. — *Powers* — By *involution*, or *powers*, is meant an operation in which a number is multiplied by itself, as $2 \times 2 = 4$, $10 \times 10 = 100$, etc.

[1] The metric system of weights and measures is described and tables are given in Chapter VIII.

The number to be multiplied by itself is called the *number;* the number by which it is multiplied is called a *factor*, and the number obtained by multiplying is called the *power*, thus:

↙ factor

$2 \times 2 = 4$ ← square, or second power.

↗

number

In algebra, which is a kind of generalized shorthand arithmetic, it is written

↙ index

$2^2 = 4$ ← square, or second power.

↗

number

where 2 is the number, ^{2} is the factor, called the *index*, and 4 is the square, or second power.

Roots. — By *evolution*, or the *extraction of roots* as it is called, is meant the operation of division whereby a number divided by another number called the factor will give another number called its root, as

↙ factor

$16 \div 4 = 4$ ← square root

↗

number

In algebra it is written

$\sqrt{16} = 4$ ← square root

radical sign ↗ ↖ number

Hence the extraction of roots is the inverse of

multiplication but it is a much more difficult operation to perform than that of involution.

Ratios and Proportions. — *Ratio* is the relation which one number or quantity bears to another number or quantity of the same kind, as 2 to 4, 3 to 5, etc.

To find the ratio is simply a matter of division, that is, one number or quantity is divided by another number or quantity, and the resulting *quotient* is the proper relation between the two numbers or quantities.

Proportion is the equality between two ratios or quotients as, 2 is to 4 as 3 is to 6, or 3 is to 4 as 75 is to 100, when the former is written

$$2 : 4 :: 3 : 6$$

and the latter $\quad 3 : 4 :: 75 : 100$

In the last named case 3 : 4 can be written $\frac{3}{4}$ and 75 : 100 can be written $\frac{75}{100}$. Then $\frac{3}{4} = \frac{75}{100}$ and this equality between the two numbers may be proved to be true because $\frac{75}{100}$ may be reduced to $\frac{3}{4}$.

The operation of proportion is largely used in business calculations. As an illustration suppose 4 yards of silk cost $1.00 and you want to find the price of 3 yards at the same rate, then

3 yds. : 4 yds. : : $? : $1.00 [1]

or $\quad \frac{3}{4} = \frac{?}{100}$

[1] In the above example in proportion a question mark is used as the symbol for the unknown term which we wish to find. In algebra x is generally used to denote unknown quantities and is a more correct mode of expression.

now cross-multiplying we have

$$300 = 4?$$

or the cost of 3 yards is equal to

$$3.00 \div 4 \text{ or } 75 \text{ cents.}$$

Practical Applications. — The every-day applications of the above ground rules and modifications are:

Percentage, which is the *rate* per hundred or the *proportion* in one hundred parts. In business percentage means the duty, interest, or allowance on a hundred. The word *percentage* is derived from the Latin *per centum*, *per* meaning *by* and *centum* meaning a *hundred.*

Interest is the per cent of money paid for the use of money borrowed or otherwise obtained. The interest to be paid may be either agreed upon or is determined by the statutes of a state.

Simple interest is the per cent to be paid a creditor for the time that the principal remains unpaid and is usually calculated on a yearly basis, a year being taken to have 12 months, of 30 days each, or 360 days.

Compound interest is the interest on the principal and the interest that remains unpaid; the new interest is reckoned on the combined amounts, when they are considered as a new principal.

Profit and Loss are the amounts gained and the amounts lost when taken together in a business transaction.

Gross Profit is the total amount received from the sale of goods without deductions of any kind over and above the cost of purchase or production.

Net Profit is the amount remaining after all expenses such as interest, insurance, transportation, etc., are deducted from the gross cost.

Loss is the difference between the gross profit and the net profit.

Reduction of Weights and Measures means to change one weight or measure into another weight or measure. This may be done by increasing or diminishing varying scales.

Increased varying scales of weight run thus: 1 ounce, 1 pound, and 1 ton; for lineal measurement, 1 inch, 1 foot, 1 yard, etc.; for liquid measurement, 1 pint, 1 quart, 1 gallon, etc. *Decreased* varying scales run $\frac{1}{2}$ ounce, $\frac{1}{3}$ pound, and $\frac{3}{4}$ ton; $\frac{1}{4}$ inch; $\frac{1}{2}$ foot, $\frac{3}{4}$ yard, etc.; and $\frac{1}{3}$ pint, $\frac{3}{4}$ quart, and $\frac{1}{2}$ gallon.

CHAPTER II

RAPID ADDITION

Learning to Add Rapidly.
The Addition Table.
Three Line Exercise.
Quick Single Column Addition.
Simultaneous Double Column Addition.
Left-Handed Two-Number Addition.
Simultaneous Three Column Addition.
Bookkeepers Check Addition.
Adding Backwards (Check Addition).
Addition with Periods.
To Check Added Work.
Lightning Addition (so-called).

WHILE there are no direct short cuts to addition unless one uses an *arithmometer* or other adding machine there is an easy way to *learn* to add, and once learned it will not only make you quick at figuring but it will aid you wonderfully in other calculations.

The method by which this can be done is very simple and if you will spend a quarter or half an hour a day on it for a month you will be amazed to find with what speed and ease and accuracy you will be able to add up any ordinary column of numbers.

This method is to learn the *addition table* just as you learned the multiplication table when you were at school; that is, so that you instantly know the sum of any two figures below ten just as you

Addition Table

1	1	1	1	1	1	1	1	1
1	2	3	4	5	6	7	8	9
2	**3**	**4**	**5**	**6**	**7**	**8**	**9**	**10**
	2	2	2	2	2	2	2	2
	2	3	4	5	6	7	8	9
	4	**5**	**6**	**7**	**8**	**9**	**10**	**11**
		3	3	3	3	3	3	3
		3	4	5	6	7	8	9
		6	**7**	**8**	**9**	**10**	**11**	**12**
			4	4	4	4	4	4
			4	5	6	7	8	9
			8	**9**	**10**	**11**	**12**	**13**
				5	5	5	5	5
				5	6	7	8	9
				10	**11**	**12**	**13**	**14**
					6	6	6	6
					6	7	8	9
					12	**13**	**14**	**15**
						7	7	7
						7	8	9
						14	**15**	**16**
							8	8
							8	9
							16	**17**
								9
								9
								18

instantly know what the product is of the same figures.

In ordinary school work children are not taught

the addition table thoroughly and for this reason very few of them ever become expert at figures. On the other hand when one takes a course in some business college the first thing he is given to do is to learn the addition table.

Learning to Add Rapidly. — There are only 45 combinations that can be formed with the nine figures and cipher, as the preceding table shows, and these must be learned *by heart.*

After learning the addition table so thoroughly you can skip around and know the sum of any of the two-figure combinations in the preceding table, then make up exercises in which three figures form a column and practice on these until you can read the sums offhand, thus:

Three Line Exercise

1	2	3	4	5	6	7	8	9
2	3	4	5	6	7	8	9	1
3	4	5	6	7	8	9	1	2
6	9	12	15	18	21	24	18	12

When you have mastered the three line combinations as given in the above exercise so that the instant you glance at any column you can give the sum of it without having to add the figures repeatedly, you should extend the exercise to include all possible combinations of three figures.

Follow this with exercises of four line figures and when you can do these without mental effort you are in a fair way to become a rapid calculator and an accurate accountant.

Quick Single Column Addition. — One of the quickest and most accurate ways of adding long columns of figures is to add each column by itself and write down the unit of the sum under the units column, the tens of the sum under the hundreds column of the example, etc. The two sums are then added together, which gives the total sum, as shown in the example on the right.

		(d)	(b)	(c)	(a)	
		9	8	7	4	
		8	7	6	5	
		3	4	2	5	
		8	2	6	7	
		5	2	7	9	
		8	7	4	2	
Third col.		3	0	3	2	first column
Fourth col.	4	1	3	2		second column
Total	4	4	3	5	2	

	38
	41
	23
	18
	34
	16
	22
	55
	66
	91
First column sum	44
Second column sum	36
Total sum	404

Where a column of three, four, or more figures, as shown in the example on the right of this page, is to be added, the separate columns are added up in the order shown by the letters in parenthesis above each column; that is, the units (a) column is added first and the sum set down as usual; the hundreds (b) column is added next and the unit figure of this sum is set under the hundreds column, which makes 3032; add the tens column next and set down the units figure of this sum under the tens column and set the tens figure of this sum under the hundreds column and finally add up the thousands column, which makes 4132. Finally add the two sums together and the total will be the sum wanted.

There are several reasons why this method of adding each column separately is better than the usual method of adding and carrying to the next column, and among these are (a) it does away with the mentally carried number; (b) a mistake is much more readily seen; and (c) the correction is confined to the sum of the column where the mistake occurred, and this greatly simplifies the operation.

Simultaneous Double Column Addition. — While accountants as a rule add one column of figures at a time as just described, many become so expert it is as easy for them to add two columns at the same time as it is one and besides it is considerably quicker.

A good way to become an adept at adding two columns at once is to begin by adding a unit number to a double column number, thus:

$$(a)\quad \begin{array}{r} 16 \\ 9 \\ \hline 25 \end{array} \qquad\qquad (b)\quad \begin{array}{r} 44 \\ 8 \\ \hline 52 \end{array}$$

The sums of any such combinations should be known the instant you see them and without the slightest hesitancy or thought.

Since the sum of the two unit figures have already been learned and as the tens figure of the units sum is never more than 1 it is easy to think, say, or write 1 more to the sum of the tens column than the figure in the tens column calls for.

For instance, 1 in the tens column of the larger number (16 in the (9) case) calls for 2 in the tens column of the sum; 3 in the tens column of the larger number calls for 4 in the tens column of the sum, etc.

Where double columns are added, as

$$\begin{array}{r} 68 \\ 87 \\ \hline 155 \end{array}$$

the mind's eye sees the sum of both the units column and the tens column at practically the same instant, thus:

$$\begin{array}{r} 68 \\ 87 \\ \hline 14\underbrace{1}5 \\ 5 \end{array}$$

carries the tens figure of the sum of the units column, which in this case is 1, and adds it to the units figure of the second sum, which in this case is 4, the total sum, which is 155, is had.

After you are sufficiently expert to rapidly add up single columns it is only a step in advance and one which is easily acquired, especially where the sum is not more than 100, to add up two columns at the same time, and following this achievement summing up three or more numbers is as easily learned.

Left-Handed Two-Number Addition. — This is a somewhat harder method of addition than the usual one but it often affords relief to an overworked mind to change methods and what is more to the point it affords an excellent practice drill.

Take as an example

$$\begin{array}{r} 492 \\ 548 \\ \hline 1040 \end{array}$$

Begin by adding the left-hand or hundreds column first, then add the tens column, and finally the units column; in the above example $5 + 4 = 10$ and a glance will show that 1 is to be carried, hence put down 10 in your grey matter for the sum on the left-hand side; $4 + 9 = 13$ and another glance at the units column shows that 1 is also to be carried and 1 added to $3 = 4$, so put down 4 for the tens column of the sum, and as $8 + 2 = 10$ and the 1 having already been carried put down 0 in the units column of the sum.

Left-hand addition is just like saying the alphabet backward — it is as much of a novelty and far more useful — in that it is just as easy to do it as the right-hand frontward way — after it is once learned.

Simultaneous Three Column Addition. —
Example. —

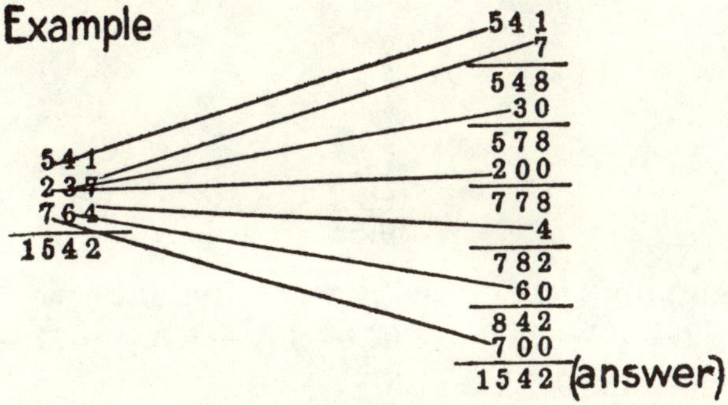

Rule. — An easy and rapid way to add three columns of figures at the same time is to take the upper number (541) and add the units figure of the next lower number (7) to it (548); then make the tens figure (3) a multiple of 10 (in this case it is 30) and add it to the first sum (548); then make the hundreds figure a multiple of 100 (in this it is 200) and add it to the last sum (778) and so on with each figure of each number to the last column, when the total will be the sum of the column.

When adding three columns of numbers by this method you can start with the lower number and add upward just as well as starting with the upper number and adding down. By adding mentally, many of the operations which are shown in the right-hand column do not appear, only the succeeding sums being noted.

This operation is especially useful in figuring up cost sums, thus:

$ .75
4.20
1.95
2.37
.25
$9.52

Beginning with the lower amount we have 25 — 32 — 62 — 262 — 267 — 357— 457 — 477 —877 — 882 — and 9.52.

Bookkeepers Check Addition. — This method is largely used by bookkeepers and others where there are apt to be interruptions since it is simple, single column addition, and as the sum of each column is set down by itself there is no carrying, hence there is small chance for errors and it can be easily checked up.

The rule is to put down separately the sum of the units column on the top right-hand side, the sum of the tens column with the unit figure under the tens figure of the first added, and so on until all of the columns have been added and their individual sums arranged in the order given, thus:

5	7	6	4	2	
7	3	2	5	4	
5	3	6	6	4	
3	9	4	3	5	26
5	2	7	1	3	32
1	6	8	4	6	39
4	3	6	9	2	33
30	33	39	32	26	30
33	7,	2	4	6	337,246

Adding Backward (Check Addition). — The sums of each of the above columns may be set down in the reverse order to that shown above; that is, with the sum of the unit column at the lower right-hand side, the sum of the tens column with the unit figure over the tens figure of the last sum, and so on until all of the sums of the separate columns have been written down in this order:

```
30
 33
  39
   32
    26
337246
```

Period Addition. — A great help in adding up long single columns is to use periods to mark off 10's; that is, the units are added up until the one is reached where the sum is just less than 20; this one is checked off with a period, or other mark which stands for 10; the amount of the sum over

10 is carried and added to the next unit and the adding goes on until the sum is again just less than 20, when this figure is checked off, and so on to the top of the column; the last sum is either mentally noted, or it can be written down and then added to the tens as indicated by the periods, when the total will be the sum of the single column.

```
7  (14)                14
4 . (17 carry 7) . = 1.0
6
3 . (17 carry 7) . = 10
5
8 . (19 carry 9) . = 10
7
1 . (14 carry 4) . = 10
6
2 . (17 carry 7) . = 10
4
3
8
--------------------------
64                     64
```

To Check Addition. — To ascertain whether or not the work that has been added is correct it should be checked up by some one of the various methods given in connection with the above examples. As good a method as any is to add each column from the bottom up and then from the top down.

Lightning Addition. — The rules given in the preceding pages cover practically all of the real helps in making addition a quick, easy, and accurate operation. To add any number of figures on sight is a delusion and a snare, a trick pure and simple, which you or any one can do when you know the secret, and as such it will be explained under the caption of *The Magic of Figures* in Chapter VIII of this book.

CHAPTER III

RAPID SUBTRACTION

The Taking-Away Method.
The Subtraction Table.
Subtraction by Addition.
Combined Addition and Subtraction.
Subtracting Two or More Numbers from Two or More Other Numbers.
To Check the Work.

It has been previously pointed out that addition and subtraction are *universal* operations and hence they are closely related.

There are two methods in use by which the difference or *remainder* between two numbers can be found and these are (1) the *taking-away*, or *complement* method, and (2) the *making-up*, or *making-change* method, as these methods are variously called.

The Taking-Away Method. — In the taking-away or complement the difference or remainder between two numbers is found by *thinking down* from the whole number, or *minuend*, to the smaller number, or *subtrahend*.

The difference between two numbers, or remainder, is called the *complement* for the simple reason that it completes what the subtrahend lacks to make up the minuend; thus in subtracting 4 from 9 the remainder is 5 and hence 5 is the complement of 4.

When subtraction is performed by the taking away, or complement method, the subtraction table should be thoroughly learned, and as subtraction is the inverse operation of addition, of course but 45 combinations can be made with the nine figures and the cipher and these are given in the following table:

The Subtraction Table

2								
1								
1								
3	3							
1	2							
2	1							
4	4	4						
1	2	3						
3	2	1						
5	5	5	5					
1	2	3	4					
4	3	2	1					
6	6	6	6	6				
1	2	3	4	5				
5	4	3	2	1				
7	7	7	7	7	7			
1	2	3	4	5	6			
6	5	4	3	2	1			
8	8	8	8	8	8	8		
1	2	3	4	5	6	7		
7	6	5	4	3	2	1		
9	9	9	9	9	9	9	9	
1	2	3	4	5	6	7	8	
8	7	6	5	4	3	2	1	
10	10	10	10	10	10	10	10	10
1	2	3	4	5	6	7	8	9
9	8	7	6	5	4	3	2	1

This table should be learned so that the remainder of any of the two-figure combinations given in the above table can be instantly named, and this is a very much easier thing to do than to learn the addition, since the remainder is 9; and when the table is learned letter perfect, rapid subtraction becomes a simple matter.

Subtraction by Addition. — If the subtraction table has never been thoroughly learned, then the easiest way to do subtraction is by the *making-up*, or *making-change* method, and which is also sometimes called the *Austrian* method. This method is very simple in that it consists of *adding* to the subtrahend a number large enough to equal the minuend.

For example, suppose a customer has bought an article for 22 cents and he hands the clerk a $1.00 bill. In giving him his change the clerk hands him 3 pennies and says "25"; then he hands him a quarter and says "50," and finally he hands him a half-dollar and says "and 50 makes $1.00."

He has performed the operation of subtracting 22 cents from $1.00 by simple addition, since 22 cents added to 3 pennies make 25 cents, and the quarter added to the 25 cents makes 50 cents and the half-dollar added to the 50 cents makes up the dollar, or worked out in simple figures it becomes

$$\underset{\text{subtrahend}\ \nearrow}{22} + \underbrace{3 + 25 + 50}_{.78\ \leftarrow\ \text{remainder}} = \underset{\nwarrow\ \text{minuend}}{\$1.00}$$

or to do it by the complement method, then

$1.00	amount tendered
.22	amount purchased
.78	difference returned in change.

Combined Addition and Subtraction. — In business calculations it is often necessary to add two or more numbers and then subtract the sum of them from another number. When this is the case the operations of addition and subtraction need not be performed separately but they may be done in one operation.

Suppose, by way of illustration, that you have a certain balance in the bank to your credit and you have made, let us say, four checks against it, and that you want to know what the balance is after the amounts of the checks have been deducted, thus:

$462.76	original balance
3.80	checks drawn
16.50	
12.16	
7.69	
422.61	new balance

In this operation each column of the checks drawn is added and the unit of the sum is subtracted from the corresponding column of the amount of the original balance and the remainder is put down under this column for the new balance.

In the above example, for instance, the 6 and

9 of the units column of the checks drawn are added, making 15, and the 5 of the latter number is subtracted from the 6 of the units column of the original balance, and 1 is put down in the units column of the new balance.

The 1 from the 15 is carried and added to the tens column of the checks drawn, which makes 21, and the 1 of the latter is subtracted from the 7 in the tens column of the original balance and the remainder, 6, is put down in the tens column of the new balance.

Next the 2 of the added tens column is carried and added to the hundreds column of the checks drawn, which makes 20, and the cipher subtracted from the 2 of the original balance leaves 2, which is put down in the hundreds column of the new balance.

Finally the 2 of the added hundreds column is carried and added to the thousands column, making 4, and this subtracted from 6 in the thousands column of the original balance leaves 2, which is set down in the thousands column of the new balance, and putting down the remaining 4 of the original balance a new balance is had of $422.61.

Subtracting Two or More Numbers from Two or More Other Numbers. — There are often cases where two or more numbers have to be subtracted from two or more other numbers, and this can be easily and quickly done by an extension of the method just given.

Suppose you have made deposits for each day in the week excluding Sunday, and on each day of the week you have made certain checks; as an example, say that your deposits and checks have run for a week like this:

Mon.	$27.82	
Tues.	33.46	
Wed.	17.25	Deposits
Thurs.	48.21	
Fri.	19.25	
Sat.	35.45	
Mon.	$10.20	
	15.35	
	32.01	Checks Made
	7.16	
	11.25	
	35.45	
	70.02	Balance
	181.44	total deposits
	111.42	total checks
	70.02	balance

In this case add up the units column of the *deposits first* and then add up the units column of the checks, subtract the latter from the former number and put down the units figure, which is 2, in the units column; carry the tens figure, which is 2, of the units column of the deposits and add it to the tens column of the deposits. Then carry the tens figure of the unit column of the checks drawn, which is 1, and add it to the tens column of the deposits and subtract as before, and so on until all of the columns of both deposits and checks drawn have been added separately and subtracted and the remainders put down.

To Check the Work. — To check the results of subtraction all that is needed is to add the remainder and the subtrahend together and the sum of these two numbers will be the same as the minuend, that is, if the answer is right.

CHAPTER IV

SHORT CUTS IN MULTIPLICATION

The Multiplication Table

(1) A Further Extension of the Multiplication Table.
(2) To Find the Square of Two Numbers when Both End in 5.
(3) To Find the Product of Two Numbers when Both End in 5 and the Tens Figures are even.
(4) To Find the Product of Two Numbers when Both End in 5 and the Tens Figures are Uneven.
(5) To Multiply any Number by 10, 100, 1000, etc.
(6) To Multiply Any Number by a Multiple of 10, as 20, 300, 4000, etc.
(7) To Multiply any Number Ending in Ciphers by a Multiple of 10.
(8) To Multiply any Number by 25 or 75.
(9) To Multiply any Number by Higher Multiples of 25, as 125, 250, etc.
(10) To Square Any Number Formed of Nines.
(11) To Multiply a Number by 11 or Any Multiple of 11, as 22, 33, 44, etc.
(12) To Multiply a Number by 21, 31, 41, etc.
(13) To Multiply a Number by 101, 201, 301, etc.
(14) To Square a Number Having Two Figures.
(15) To Multiply any Two Numbers of Two Figures Each where the Units are Alike.
(16) To Multiply any Two Numbers of Two Figures Each where the Tens are Alike.
(17) To Multiply any Number by a Number Formed of Factors.
(18) The Complement Method of Multiplying.
(19) The Supplement Method of Multiplying.
(20) The Sliding Method of Multiplying.

To Check the Work:

Check I. — By Division
II. — By Division
III. — By Casting Out Nines
IV. — Lightning Method.

To become an adept at short cuts in arithmetic the multiplication table must be so well learned that the product of any two numbers up to and including 12 may be instantly expressed without thinking.

After the table is learned — indeed there are very few who are not already proficient — the next step is to know the short-cut rules and how to form certain number combinations, and then — *practice* until you have mastered them.

When these principles are followed you will be able to solve a large number of arithmetical problems with lightning-like rapidity.

The Multiplication Table

1	2	3	4	5	6	7	8	9	10	11	12	13	14	15	**1**
2	**4**	6	8	10	12	14	16	18	20	22	24	26	28	30	**2**
3	6	**9**	12	15	18	21	24	27	30	33	36	39	24	45	**3**
4	8	12	**16**	20	24	28	32	36	40	44	48	52	56	60	**4**
5	10	15	20	**25**	30	35	40	45	50	55	60	65	70	75	**5**
6	12	18	24	30	**36**	42	48	54	60	66	72	78	84	90	**6**
7	14	21	28	3	42	**49**	56	63	70	77	84	91	98	105	**7**
8	16	24	32	40	48	56	**64**	72	80	88	96	104	112	120	**8**
9	18	27	36	45	54	63	72	**81**	90	99	108	117	126	135	**9**
10	20	30	40	50	60	70	80	90	**100**	110	120	130	140	150	**10**
11	22	33	44	55	66	77	88	99	110	**121**	132	143	154	165	**11**
12	24	36	48	60	72	84	96	108	120	132	**144**	156	168	180	**12**
13	26	39	52	65	78	91	104	117	130	143	156	**169**	182	195	**13**
14	28	42	56	70	84	98	112	126	140	154	168	182	**196**	210	**14**
15	30	45	60	75	90	105	120	135	150	165	180	195	210	**225**	**15**

Having mastered the multiplication table you are provided with a mental master-key which will quickly unlock any of the following short-cut rules.

(1) A Further Extension of the Multiplication Table. — *Multiplying by the Teens.*

Example: $18 \times 15 = 270$ (Answer)

Rule. — To the multiplicand add the unit figure of the multiplier and annex a cipher; to this add the product obtained by multiplying the unit figures of both the multiplier and the multiplicand, thus:

$$18 + 5 = 23 \text{ or annexing a cipher}$$
$$= 230$$
$$5 \times 8 = 40 \text{ or}$$
$$230 + 40 = 270 \text{ (Answer)}$$

(2) To Find the Square of Two Numbers when Both End in 5.

Example: $25 \times 25 = 625$

Rule. — (*a*) Multiply the 5's in the units column and write down 25 for the ending figures of the product; (*b*) add 1 to the first 2 (or other figure) in the tens column which makes 3 and then (*c*) multiply the 3 by the 2 in the other tens column thus:

$$25 \times 25 =$$
$$5 \times 5 = 25$$
$$2 \times 3 = \underline{6}$$
$$625 \text{ (Answer)}$$

(3) To Find the Product of Two Numbers when Both End in 5 and the Tens Figures are Even.

Example: $25 \times 45 = 1125$

Rule. — (*a*) Multiply the 5's in the units column as before and write down 25 for the ending figures of the product; (*b*) add the figures of the tens column (in the above example $2 + 4 = 6$) and (*c*) divide the sum (6) by 2; (*d*) multiply the two figures in the tens column ($2 \times 4 = 8$) and (*e*) add the remainder ($6 \div 2 = 3$) which will give the last figure of the product (11) thus:

	$25 \times 45 =$	
(*a*)	$5 \times 5 =$	25
(*b*)	$2 + 4 = 6$	
(*c*)	$6 \div 2 = 3$	
(*d*)	$2 \times 4 = 8$	
(*e*)	$3 + 8 =$	11
		1125 (Answer)

(4) To Find the Product of Two Numbers when Both End in 5 and the Tens Figures are Uneven.

Example: $35 \times 65 = 2275$

Rule. — (*a*) Where the tens figures are odd (as 3 and 6) write down 75 for the ending figures of the product; (*b*) add the tens figures ($3 + 6 = 9$), (*c*) divide the sum (9) by 2 (which gives $4\frac{1}{2}$), (*d*) leave off the fraction and add the quotient (4) to (*e*) the product found by multiplying the figures of the tens columns ($3 \times 6 = 18$) and write the result (22) before the 75, thus:

$35 \times 65 = 2275$

(*a*) 5×5 write down 75
(*b*) $3 + 6 = 9$
(*c*) $9 \div 2 = 4\frac{1}{2}$
(*d*) $3 \times 6 = 18$
(*e*) $4 + 18 = 22$

$$\begin{array}{r} 22 \\ \hline 2275 \end{array}$$

(5) To Multiply any Number by 10, 100, 1000, etc. — This is the simplest of all short methods of multiplication.

Examples:

824×10
824×100
824×1000

Rule. — Annex as many ciphers as there are ciphers in the multiplier, thus:

$824 \times 1\mathit{0} = 824\mathit{0}$
↖one cipher↗

$824 \times 1\mathit{00} = 824\mathit{00}$
↖two ciphers↗

$824 \times 1\mathit{000} = 824\mathit{000}$
↖three ciphers↗

(6) To Multiply Any Number by a Multiple of 10, as 20, 300, 4000, etc.

Examples:

49×20
732×300
841×2000

Rule. — Multiply the multiplicand by the first figure of the multiplier and annex as many ciphers to the product as there are ciphers in the multipliers, thus:

49	732	841
2	3	2
980	219,600	1,682,000

(7) To Multiply any Number Ending in Ciphers by a Multiple of 10.

Examples:

$$240 \times 20 = 4{,}800$$
$$3{,}200 \times 600 = 1{,}920{,}000$$
$$5{,}000 \times 3{,}000 = 15{,}000{,}000$$

Rule. — Disregard the ciphers in the multiplicand and multiply the figures of it by the figures of the multiplier and annex as many ciphers to the product as there are ciphers in the multiplicand and the multiplier together, thus:

24	32	5
2	6	3
4800	1,920,000	15,000,000

(8) To Multiply any Number by 25 or 75. — In this short cut the desired product is obtained by *division.*

Examples: (*a*) $219 \times 25 = 5{,}475$

(*b*) $523 \times 75 = 4{,}025$

Rule A. — First be it known that

$$100 \div 25 = 4$$

and

$$100 \div 75 = \tfrac{3}{4}$$

In the above examples annex two ciphers to the multiplicand, thus:

(*a*) 21900
(*b*) 52300

Now in example (*a*) since $100 \div 25 = 4$, by dividing 21900 by 4 gives the same result as multiplying 219 by 25, thus:

$$(a)\quad 4 \,\underline{|\,21900}$$
$$5475 \text{ (Answer)}$$

Rule B. — Add two ciphers to the multiplicand as explained in Rule *A*, and since 75 is $\frac{3}{4}$ of 100 divide the multiplicand by 4 and then multiply the quotient by 3, thus:

$$4 \,\underline{|\,52300}$$
$$13075$$
$$\underline{\quad 3}$$
$$39225 \text{ (Answer)}$$

(9) To Multiply Any Number by Higher Multiples of 25.

Examples: (*a*) 334 × 125
(*b*) 642 × 250

Rule. — Where multiples of 25 larger than 75 are used as the multipliers three ciphers are annexed to the multiplicand, and the multiplier is divided by 1000, thus in example (*a*)

$$1000 \div 125 = 8$$

and by dividing the multiplicand by 8 we get

$$(a)\quad 8 \,\underline{|\,334{,}000}$$
$$41{,}750 \text{ (Answer)}$$

In example (*b*)

$$1000 \div 250 = 4$$

and by the same operation we have

(*a*) 4 | 642,000
160,500 (Answer)

(10) To Square any Number Formed of Nines.

Example: 999 = 998001
9,999 = 99980001 (Answers)
99,999 = 9999800001

Rule. — Put down from left to right as many nines less one as the number to be squared contains, one 8 as many ciphers as there are nines in the answer and annex a 1.

(11) To Multiply a Number by 11 or Any Multiple of 11.

Examples: (*a*) $592 \times 11 = 6,512$
(*b*) $643 \times 33 = 21,219$

Rule A. — Where 11 is used as the multiplier, write down the multiplicand and under it write down the multiplicand over again but with the units column under the tens column of the first number, and then add the two numbers, thus:

(*a*) 592
592
6512 (Answer)

Rule B. — Where a higher multiple of 11 is used, as the multiplier of 33, 44, 66, write the number of the multiplicand down twice as explained in Rule *A*, add them together and then multiply the sum by 3, 4, 6, or other unit of the multiplier as the case may be, thus:

$$
\begin{array}{lr}
(b) & 643 \\
 & \underline{643} \\
 & 7073 \\
 & \underline{3} \\
 & 21219 \text{ (Answer)}
\end{array}
$$

(12) To Multiply a Number by 21, 31, 41, etc.

Example: 342 × 81 = 27,702

Rule. — (*a*) First write down the unit figure of the multiplicand (which in this case is 2) for the unit figure of the answer; (*b*) multiply the unit figure of the multiplicand by the tens figure of the multiplier (8 × 2 = 16); (*c*) add the product (16) to the tens figure of the multiplicand (4 + 16 = 20); (*d*) set down the unit figure of the sum (0) in the answer and carry the tens figure (2); (*e*) then multiply the tens figures of both multiplicand and multiplier (8 × 4 = 32); (*f*) add now the tens figure of the sum carried (2) to the product above (32 + 2 = 34).

(*g*) Add the hundreds in the multiplicand (3) to the above sum (34 + 3 = 37); (*h*) and set down the unit figure of this sum (7) in the answer and carry the tens figure (3); (*i*) multiply the hundreds figure of the multiplicand (3) by the tens figure of the multiplier (8 × 3= 24); (*j*) add the figure carried (3 + 24 = 27), and as this is the last operation (*k*) set down the sum (27) before the first figures of the product and this will be the answers.

While this may seem a long rule it is quite simple and once put into actual practice any number can be multiplied by any number less than 100, if it ends in 1, with great rapidity.

Following the rule step by step in figures it works thus:

(*a*) write down **2** for the answer
(*b*) $8 \times 2 = 16$
(*c*) $4 + 16 = 20$
(*d*) write down **0** for the answer
(*e*) $8 \times 4 = 32$
(*f*) $32 + 2 = 34$
(*g*) $34 + 3 = 37$
(*h*) write down **7** for the answer
(*i*) $8 \times 3 = 24$
(*j*) $3 + 24 = 27$
(*k*) write down **27** for the answer

27702 (Answer)

(13) To Multiply a Number by 101, 301, 501, etc.

Example: $536 \times 401 = 214936$

Rule. — (*a*) Put down the unit and tens figures of the multiplicand (36) for the answer; (*b*) multiply the unit figure of the multiplicand and the hundreds figure of the multiplier ($6 \times 4 = 24$); (*c*) add the sum (24) and the hundreds figure of the multiplicand ($24 + 5 = 29$); (*d*) put down the unit figure of this sum (9) and carry the tens figure (2); (*e*) multiply the tens and hundreds figures of the multiplicand (53) by the hundreds figure of the multiplier ($4 \times 53 = 212$); (*f*) to this sum (212) add the carried figure ($212 + 2 = 214$); (*g*) write down the last sum (214) in the result and this will be the answer (214,936).

The rule works out in figures thus:

(*a*) put down 36 for the answer
(*b*) $6 \times 4 = 24$
(*c*) $24 \times 5 = 29$
(*d*) put down 9 and carry 2
(*e*) $4 \times 53 = 212$
(*f*) $212 + 2 = 214$
(*g*) write down 214 for the answer

214,936 (Answer)

(14) To Square a Number Having Two Figures.

Example: $73 \times 73 = 5329$

Rule A. — (*a*) Multiply the unit figure of the multiplicand (3) by the unit figure of the multiplier ($3 \times 3 = 9$) and write down the product; (*b*) add the unit figure of the multiplicand (3) and that of the multiplier ($3 + 3 = 6$); (*c*) multiply one of the tens figures (7) by the last sum ($7 \times 6 = 42$); (*d*) write down the unit of the product (2) and carry the tens (4); (*e*) multiply the tens figures together ($7 \times 7 = 49$); (*f*) and add the figure carried ($49 + 4 = 53$) and write down this last sum (53) for the answer, thus:

5329

or (*a*) $3 \times 3 = 9$

write down the **9**

(*b*) $3 + 3 = 6$

(*c*) $7 + 6 = 42$

(*d*) put down **2** and carry **4**

(*e*) $7 + 7 = 49$

(*f*) $49 + 4 = 53$

write down **53**

Example: $76 \times 76 = 5772$

Rule. — Where a product larger than 9 results when the units of numbers are multiplied, and a figure remains to be carried this rule applies:

(*a*) Multiply the unit of the multiplicand (6) by the unit of the multiplier ($6 \times 6 = 36$); (*b*) write down the unit of this product (6) for the answer, and carry the tens figure (3); (*c*) add the tens figures of the multiplicand and multiplier ($7 + 7 = 14$); (*d*) multiply the sum (14) by one of the units ($14 \times 6 = 84$), (*e*) and to the latter product (84) add the carried figure ($84 + 3 = 87$); (*f*) write down the unit figure of this sum (7) for the answer, and carry the tens figure (8); (*g*) multiply the tens figures ($7 \times 7 = 49$); (*h*) add the carried figure ($49 + 8 = 57$), (*i*) and write down this sum (57) and the whole number will be the square of the numbers multiplied (5776).

The rule may be simplified thus:

(*a*) $6 \times 6 = 36$

(*b*) write down **6** and carry **3**

(*c*) $7 + 7 = 14$
(*g*) $14 \times 6 = 84$
(*e*) $84 + 3 = 87$
(*f*) write down **7** and carry **8**
(*g*) $7 \times 7 = 49$
(*h*) $49 + 8 = 57$
(*i*) write down **57**

(15) To Multiply any Two Numbers of Two Figures Each Where the Units are Alike.

Example: $53 \times 63 = 3339$

Rule. — (*a*) Multiply the unit figures ($3 \times 3 = 9$); (*b*) and write down the product (9) for the answer; (*c*) add the tens figures ($5 + 6 = 11$); (*d*) multiply the sum (11) by one of the units ($11 \times 3 = 33$); (*e*) write down the unit of this sum (3) for the answer and carry the tens figure (3); (*f*) multiply the tens figures ($5 \times 6 = 30$); (*g*) add this product (30) to the carried figure ($30 + 3 = 33$), (*h*) and write down this sum (33), when the whole number will be the answer (3339); or simplified it becomes:

(*a*) $3 \times 3 = 9$
(*b*) write down the **9**
(*c*) $5 + 6 = 11$
(*d*) $11 \times 3 = 33$
(*e*) write down **3** and carry **3**
(*f*) $5 \times 6 = 30$
(*g*) $30 + 3 = 33$
(*h*) write down **33**

(16) To Multiply any Two Numbers of Two Figures Each Where the Tens are Alike.

Example: $42 \times 45 = 1890$

Rule. — (*a*) Multiply the unit figures ($5 \times 2 = 10$); (*b*) write down the unit of the sum (0) and carry the tens figure (1); (*c*) add the unit figures ($5 + 2 = 7$); (*d*) multiply this sum (7) by one of the tens figures ($4 \times 7 = 28$); (*e*) add the product (28) to the figure carried ($28 + 1 = 29$); (*f*) write down the unit figure of the sum (9) and carry the tens figure (2); (*g*) multiply the tens figures ($4 \times 4 = 16$); (*h*) add the product (16) to the carried figure ($16 + 2 = 18$), (*i*) and write the sum (18) for the answer (1890); or it may be written thus:

(*a*) $5 \times 2 = 10$
(*b*) write 0 and carry 1
(*c*) $5 + 2 = 7$
(*d*) $7 \times 4 = 28$
(*e*) $28 + 1 = 29$
(*f*) write 9 and carry 2
(*g*) $4 \times 4 = 16$
(*h*) $16 + 2 = 18$

(17) To Multiply any Number by a Number Formed of Factors.

Example: $384 \times 648 = 248832$

Rule A. — In this case 64 can be factored by 8, that is $8 \times 8 = 64$. (*a*) Multiply the multiplicand (384) by the unit figure of the multiplier ($8 \times 384 =$

3072; (*b*) now since 8 is a factor of 64 multiply the last product (3072) by one of the factors (3072 × 24576); (*c*) put down this product so that the unit figure (6) will be under the tens column of the first product (7) and add the two products and the sum will be the product of the two numbers.

Worked out the operations are:

```
      384               3072               3072
(a)     8     (b)          8      (c)  24576
     3072              24576           248832 (Answer)

or                       384
                         648
                        3072
                       24576
                      248832 (Answer)
```

Example: 485 × 432 = 209,520

Rule B. — In this case 32 can be factored, since 4 × 8 = 32. (*a*) Multiply the multiplicand (485) by the hundreds figure of the multiplier (4 × 485 = 1940); (*b*) now since 8 is a factor of 32 multiply this product (1940) by 8 which gives 15520; (*c*) write the last product (15520) two figures to the right of the first product (1940) and add, when the sum will be the product wanted, thus:

```
      485              1940            1940
(a)   4 4     (b)         8     (c)      15520
     1940             15520         209,520   (Answer)
```

or
```
   485
   432
  ----
  1940
 15520
 -----
209,520 (Answer)
```

(18) The Complement Method of Multiplying.

Example: $93 \times 95 = 8835$

Rule. — The *complement* of a number is the figure required to bring it up to 100 or some multiple of 100; thus 5 is the complement of 95 and 7 is the complement of 93.

(*a*) Multiply the complements of the two numbers ($7 \times 5 = 35$) and (*b*) write down the product (35) for the answer; (*c*) subtract either complement from either number (say $93 - 5 = 88$) and (*d*) write down the remainder for the answer (88), thus:

```
93 × 95 = 8835
 7    5 → complement
  ↖ complement
```

(*a*) $7 \times 5 =$ **35**

(*b*) write down 35 for the answer

(*c*) $93 - 5 =$ **88**

(*d*) write down 88 for the answer

which is 8835 (Answer)

(19) The Supplement Method of Multiplying.

Example: $106 \times 105 = 11130$

Rule. — The supplement of a number is its unit figure over 100; thus 6 is the supplement of 100 and 5 is the supplement of 105.

(*a*) Multiply the first two units of the numbers ($6 \times 5 = 30$) and (*b*) write down the product (30) for the last figures of the answer; (*c*) add the supplement of either number to the other number ($106 + 5 = 111$), and (*d*) write down the sum (111) for the first figures of the answer, thus:

(*a*) $6 \times 5 = 30$
(*b*) write down **30** for the answer
(*c*) $106 + 5 = 111$
(*d*) write down **111** for the answer

which is 11130 (Answer)

(20) The Sliding Method of Multiplying.

Example: $324 \times 123 = 39{,}852$

Rule. — To multiply by the sliding method it is necessary to write the two numbers on separate slips of paper. As an illustration in the above example the multiplicand, or larger number, is written in the reverse order, as 423 instead of 324.

Now place the slips of paper one under the other so that the problem looks like this:

```
      423
    123
    ---
```

Next multiply the 4 by the 3 thus: $4 \times 3 = 12$, set down the 2 down in the answer, and carry the 1; slide the upper number along until the figures are in this order:

```
      423
     123
     ---
```

Multiply the 4 by the 2 and the 2 by the 3 thus: $4 \times 2 = 8$ and $2 \times 3 = 6$. Add these products and the 1 which was carried from above thus: $6 + 8 + 1 = 15$. Put down the 5 in the answer and carry the 1, and slide the upper numbers along until they bear this relation:

$$\begin{array}{r} 423 \\ \underline{123} \end{array}$$

This time multiply all three sets of numbers, thus $4 \times 1 = 4$, $2 \times 2 = 4$, and $3 \times 3 = 9$. Add these products and the 1 which was carried from the above thus: $4 + 4 + 9 + 1 = 18$; write the 8 down in the answer and carry the 1, and slide the upper slip along until the numbers are in this position:

$$\begin{array}{r} 423 \\ \underline{123} \end{array}$$

Multiply the 2 by 1 and the 3 by 2 thus: $2 \times 1 = 2$ and $3 \times 2 = 6$. To the sum of these products add the 1 carried from above thus: $2 + 6 + 1 = 9$; set the 9 down in the answer and again slide the upper slip until the numbers are thus arranged:

$$\begin{array}{l} 423 \\ \underline{123} \end{array}$$

Finally multiply the 3 by the 1 and write the product down in the answer and when this is done we have as the product:

$$324 \times 123 = 39{,}852 \text{ (Answer)}$$

To Check the Work. — There are several ways to check up products in multiplication but the following are the shortest and best.

Check I. — *By Division.*

Example: $32 \times 58 = 1856$

Check: $1856 \div 58 = 32$

Rule. — Divide the product by the multiplier and the quotient will be the multiplicand.

Check II. — *By Division.*

Example: $9 \times 8 \times 2 \times 7 \times 5 = 5040$

Check: $5040 \div 9 = 560 = 8 \times 2 \times 7 \times 5$

Rule. — Divide the product by one of the factors, when the quotient should be equal to the product of the remaining factors.

Check III. — *By Casting out the Nines.*

Example:

$$\begin{array}{rl} 34 & = 7 \\ \underline{26} & = \underline{8} \\ 204 & \ 56 = \mathbf{2} \\ \underline{68} & \\ 884 & = \mathbf{2} \end{array}$$

The example is proved as follows by *casting out* the nines, that is to take out all the nines contained in the multiplicand and using the remainders.

First Step. — Cast out the nines in the multiplicand and set down the remainder, or excess of nines. Since in this case there are three nines in the multiplicand and $3 \times 9 = 27$ then the remainder will be equal to $34 - 27$ or 7.

Second Step. — Cast out the nines in the multiplier and set down the remainder. There are two nines in 26 and since 2 × 9 = 18 the remainder is equal to 26 – 18 or 8.

Third Step. — Multiply the remainders by each other: In the above example 7 × 8 = 56, and cast the nines out of the product thus obtained. In this case there are 6 nines in 56 and since 9 × 6 = 54 the remainder = 56 – 54 or 2.

Fourth Step. — Now cast the nines out of the answer. In this case there are 98 nines in the answer and since 9 × 98 = 882 then the remainder is 884 – 882 or 2. And since the product of the excesses of nine is 56 and the excess of nines in 56 is 2 and the excess of nines in the answer is 2 the work is proved correct.

Check IV. The Lightning Method. — A simple way of proving multiplication with lightninglike rapidity is based on casting out the nines. It is also called the method of *unitates.* Now the unitate of a number is the sum of the figures which make up the number reduced to one figure, thus:

number		sum		sum reduced		unitate
347653	=	28	=	10	=	1
503792	=	26	=			8
437965	=	34	=			7

The sum of the figures in 347653 is 28; by adding the figures in 28 we have 10 and adding the figures in 10 we get 1.

The way in which the method of unitates is applied to checking multiplication is as follows:

Example 1:

```
     432  =  9 )
     331  =  7 } 63  =  9
     432
    1296
   1296
 142,992  = 27         =  9
```

In this example the unitate of the multiplicand (432) is 9 and the unitate of the multiplier (331) is 7. Now multiplying these unitates we have $9 \times 7 = 63$ and the unitate of 63 is 9.

An examination of the product shows that the sum of the figures comprising it is 27 and the unitate of 27 is 9. Therefore since the unitate of the product, multiplier, and the multiplicand is 9 also, the work must be correct.

Example 2:

```
    459  = 18 =  9 )
    230  =       5 } = 45 = 9
  13770
   918
105,570  =      18    = 9
```

The simplicity of this check makes it easily used and hence it should be done mentally.

CHAPTER V

SHORT CUTS IN DIVISION

To Instantly Find the Divisor of a Number.
To Divide Any Number by 10, 100, 1000, etc.
To Divide a Number by 25 or a Multiple of 25, as 5, 75, 125, etc.
To Divide a Number by a Number Formed of Factors (where there are no Remainders).
To Divide a Number by a Number Formed of Factors (where there is a Remainder).
To Divide a Number by a Number Formed of Three Factors.
To Check the Work:
I. By Casting out the Nines.
II. The Lightning Method.

WHILE there are no tables to learn as an aid to short-cut division there are however a few rules which, if you know them, will instantly show what figure can be used as a divisor and hence much time and effort is saved in trying out different figures to find a divisor.

To Instantly Find the Divisor of a Number.

(*A*) An even number can, of course, always be divided by **2**, thus:

32574

(*B*) When the sum of the figures forming a number can be divided by **3** the number itself can be divided by **3**, thus:

651 $(12 \div 3 = 4)$

(*C*) When a number ends in two ciphers, or the last two numbers can be divided by **4** then the whole number can be divided by **4**, thus:

3200 or 868, because in the latter case 68 can be divided by 4.

(*D*) When a number ends with either a cipher or **5** then the number can be divided by **5**, thus:

3200 or 775

(*E*) When the number is even and the sum of the figures forming it can be divided by **3** then the number can be divided by **6**, thus:

1284 (1 + 2 + 8 + 4 = 15 and 15 ÷ 3 = 5)

(*F*) When the sum of the odd place figures of a number minus the sum of the even place figures can be divided by **7** then the whole number can be divided by **7**, thus:

↙ even place

2 2 7 2 9 (18 − 4 = 14)

↑ ↑

odd place

*See note on page 121.

(*G*) When the last three place figures of a number can be divided by **8** then the whole number can be divided by **8**, thus:

54184 (184 ÷ 8 = 23)

(*H*) When the sum of all the figures can be divided by 9 then the whole number can be divided by 9, thus:

33498 (3 + 3 + 4 + 9 + 8 = 27 and 27 ÷ 9 = 3)

(*I*) When the last figure of a number is a cipher it can, of course, always be divided by 10, thus:

39870

(*J*) When the sum of the odd place figures minus the sum of the even place figures of a number can be divided by 11, then the whole number can be divided by 11, thus:

even place

8 6 4 1 6 (8 + 4 + 6 = 18; 6 + 1 = 7;
18 − 7 = 11 and 11 ÷ 11 = 0)

odd place

(***K***) When the *sum* of the figures of a number can be divided by three *and* each of the last two figures of the number can be divided by four, then the number can be divided by 12.

4104 (4 + 1 + 0 + 4 = 9; 9 ÷ 3 = 3 and 4 ÷ 4 = 0)

(1) To Divide Any Number by 10, 100, 1000, etc.

Example: $3722 \div 10 = 372\frac{2}{10}$

Rule. — To divide any number by 10 or by a multiple of 10 it is only necessary to put a decimal point before the last figure, thus:

372.2

or $372\frac{2}{10}$

When a number is divided by 100 point off two figures with the decimal point; when dividing by 1000 point off three figures with the decimal point, etc.

(2) To Divide a Number by 25 or a Multiple of 25, as 5, 75, 125, etc.

Example: $4600 \div 25 = 184$

Rule A. — As 25 is $\frac{1}{4}$ of 100 drop the ciphers of the dividend (4600) and multiply the remaining figures (46) by 4, thus:

$$46 \times 4 = 184 \text{ (Answer)}$$

Rule B. As 50 is $\frac{1}{2}$ of 100 drop the ciphers of the dividend and multiply by 2; 75 is $\frac{3}{4}$ of 100 — drop the ciphers of the dividend, multiply the remaining figures by 4 and divide by 3; 125 is $\frac{5}{4}$ of 100 — drop the ciphers of the dividend, multiply the remaining figures by 4 and divide the product by 5.

(3) To Divide Any Number by a Number Formed of Factors. — *Where there are no remainders.*

Example: $12775 \div 35 = 365$

Rule. — $5 \times 7 = 35$, hence 5 and 7 are factors of 35. Divide the dividend (12775) by one of the factors (5) and divide the quotient (2555) by the other factor (7) and this quotient (365) will be the answer. In other words the example is done by two operations of short division instead of one operation of long division, thus:

$$\begin{array}{r|l} 5 & 12775 \\ \hline 7 & 2555 \\ \hline & 365 \text{ (Answer)} \end{array}$$

(4) To Divide Any Number by a Number Formed of Factors. — *Where there is a Remainder.*

Example: $4331 \div 25 = 173\frac{6}{25}$

Rule. — $5 \times 5 = 25$. Divide the dividend (4331) by one of the factors (5) and divide the quotient (846) by the other factor (5). Multiply the *second* remainder (in this example it is 1) by the first divisor (5 or $5 \times 1 = 5$) and add the *first* remainder (1) to this product (5 or $5 + 1 = 6$); using this sum (6) for the upper fraction and the divisor (25) for the lower part of the fraction ($\frac{6}{25}$) and adding this fraction to the last quotient (173) we get the answer ($173\frac{6}{25}$), thus:

first divisor → 5	4331	
5	866	1 (first remainder)
	173	1 (second remainder)

and by the above rule the remainders give 6 and by writing this over the 25 we get the full result:

$173\frac{6}{25}$ (Answer)

(5) To Divide Any Number by a Number Formed of Three Factors.

Example: $703025 \div 126 = 5579\frac{71}{126}$

Rule. — The factors of 126 are 2, 7, and 9 because $2 \times 7 \times 9 = 126$. Divide the dividend by the first factor (2, which in this case gives a quotient of 351512 with a remainder of 1); next divide this quotient (351512) by the second factor (7, which gives in this example a quotient of 50216 with no remainder); and finally divide the last quotient (50216) by the third factor (9, which gives a quotient of 5579 with a remainder of 5), thus:

First divisor →	2	703025	
Second divisor →	7	351512	1 ← first remainder
Third divisor →	9	50216	0 ← second remainder
		5579	5 ← third remainder

In order to find the real quotient of the dividend multiply the third remainder (5) by the first two divisors ($5 \times 2 \times 7 = 70$); multiply the second remainder (0) by the first divisor ($2 \times 0 = 0$) and now add the first remainder (1) to the sum of the two products just obtained, thus:

$$70 + 0 + 1 = 71$$

and since 126 is the divisor the remainder is $\frac{71}{126}$ and hence the full result is

$$5579\tfrac{71}{126} \text{ (Answer)}$$

To Check the Work. — The two following methods for checking results in division are short and good.

Check I. By Casting out the Nines.

Example: $9771 \div 232 = 42\frac{27}{232}$

or $9771 = 232 + 27$

By the same process of casting out the nines as for the multiplication check, see page 39, we have:

dividend → 9771 = 6 which is the excess of nines in 9771
divisor → 232 = 7 which is the excess of nines in 232
quotient → 42 = 6 which is the excess of nines in 42
remainder → 27 = 0

Now by multiplying the excess of nines in the divisor by those in the quotient and adding the excess of nines in the remainder then —

$$6 \times 7 + 0 = 42$$

and since the excess of nines in 42 is 6 and the excess of nines in the dividend is 6 the work is correct.

Check II. The Lightning Method. — This check was devised by Virgil D. Collins and is based on the method of casting out nines, or the *unitate method* as explained in the *Lightning Check of Multiplication.*

Example: $9771 \div 232 = 42\frac{27}{232}$

Now taking the unitates we have —

9771 = 6 which is the unitate of 9771
232 = 7 " " " 232
42 = 6 " " " 42 and
27 = 9 " " " 27

Now since this method is based on the casting out of nines, whenever we get 9 as a unitate it is called a cipher, thus:

$$27 = 9 = 0$$

Next multiplying the unitate of the divisor by

the unitate of the quotient and adding the unitate of the remainder we have —

$$6 \times 7 + 0 = 42$$

and since the unitate of 42 is 6 and the unitate of 9771 is 6, the division is proved correct. All of these operations should of course be done mentally in order to do the work with lightninglike rapidity.

Explanation of Rule F, page 57:

This rule applies only when it is possible to subtract *arithmetically* and NOT ALGEBRAICALLY, the sum of the even place figures from the sum of the odd place figures.

CHAPTER VI

SHORT CUTS IN FRACTIONS

Aliquot Parts:
- Table A
  - " B
  - " C

Decimals:
- To Change a Common Fraction into a Decimal
- Addition of Decimals
- Subtraction of Decimals
- Multiplication of Decimals
- Figuring Percentage by Decimals
- Division of Decimals:
  - To Divide a Whole Number into a Whole Number when there is a Remainder
  - To Divide a Decimal into a Whole Number
- To Change a Decimal into a Common Fraction

Aliquot Parts. — In the business world one of the chief uses of common fractions is in working out examples in which *aliquot parts* are concerned.

1. An aliquot part is a number which is contained in another number an exact number of times, and since our money system is based on 100 the aliquot parts of $1.00 are very largely used.

The aliquot parts of 100 which consist of whole numbers are 2, 4, 5, 10, 20, 25, and 50 and hence —

Table A

Aliquot Part		Equivalent Parts		Whole Number
2	is	$\frac{1}{50}$	of	100
4	"	$\frac{1}{25}$	"	100
5	"	$\frac{1}{20}$	"	100
10	"	$\frac{1}{10}$	"	100
20	"	$\frac{1}{5}$	"	100
25	"	$\frac{1}{4}$	"	100
50	"	$\frac{1}{2}$	"	100

2. Another kind of aliquot parts of 100 consists of mixed numbers. It will be seen from the following table that the numerators of the fractions representing the *equivalent parts* are in each case 1.

Table B

Aliquot Parts		Equivalent Parts		Whole Number
$6\frac{1}{4}$	is	$\frac{1}{16}$	of	100
$6\frac{2}{3}$	"	$\frac{1}{15}$	"	100
$8\frac{1}{3}$	"	$\frac{1}{12}$	"	100
$12\frac{1}{2}$	"	$\frac{1}{8}$	"	100
$16\frac{2}{3}$	"	$\frac{1}{6}$	"	100
$33\frac{1}{3}$	"	$\frac{1}{3}$	"	100

Examples: Quantity		Cents		Dollars	Solutions: Equivalent Parts Lower Half				Ans.
32	×	$6\frac{1}{4}$	=	2.00	3200	÷	16	=	\$2.00
45	×	$6\frac{2}{3}$	=	3.00	4500	÷	15	=	3.00
24	×	$8\frac{1}{3}$	=	2.00	2400	÷	12	=	2.00
64	×	$12\frac{1}{2}$	=	8.00	6400	÷	8	=	8.00
36	×	$16\frac{1}{6}$	=	6.00	3600	÷	6	=	6.00
42	×	$33\frac{1}{3}$	=	14.00	4200	÷	3	=	14.00

Rule A. — To multiply any number by any one of the aliquot parts given in Table II, simply annex two ciphers to the first number and divide it by the lower part of the fraction of the equivalent part; thus since the lower part of the equivalent part of $12\frac{1}{2}$ is 8 the number representing the quantity 64 is divided by 8 after two ciphers have been annexed to it, which makes it 6400, thus:

$$64 \times 12\tfrac{1}{2} = 800$$
$$6400 \div 6 = 800$$

3. A third class of aliquot parts is where the upper part of the equivalent fractions are larger than 1, as shown in the following table:

Table C

Aliquot Parts		Equivalent Parts		Whole Number
$13\frac{1}{3}$	is	$\frac{2}{15}$	=	100
$53\frac{1}{3}$	"	$\frac{8}{15}$	=	100
$62\frac{1}{2}$	"	$\frac{5}{8}$	=	100
$66\frac{2}{3}$	"	$\frac{2}{3}$	=	100

Examples: Quantity		Cents		Dollars	Solutions: Equivalent Fraction Lower Part				Equivalent Fraction Upper Part		Ans.
45	×	$13\frac{1}{2}$	=	600	4500 ÷	15	=	300 ×	2	=	6.00
450	×	$53\frac{1}{3}$	=	24000	45000 ÷	15	=	3000 ×	8	=	24.00
40	×	$62\frac{1}{2}$	=	2500	4000 ÷	8	=	500 ×	5	=	25.00
18	×	$66\frac{2}{3}$	=	1200	1800 ÷	3	=	600 ×	2	=	12.00

Rule B. — To multiply any mixed number by an aliquot part of 100 shown in Table 3 simply add two ciphers to the number, divide it by the lower half of the equivalent fraction and multiply the quotient thus obtained by the upper half of the equivalent fraction, thus:

$$18 \times 66\tfrac{2}{3} = 1200$$
$$1800 \div 3 = 600 \times 2 = 1200 \text{ (Answer)}$$

DECIMALS

Very often it is a decided short cut in working an example to change a common fraction into a decimal fraction, or *decimal* as it is called for short.

To Change a Common Fraction into a Decimal.

Example: $\frac{3}{4} = .75$ or $\frac{75}{100}$

General Rule. — Divide the denominator or lower part of the fraction into the numerator, or upper part of the fraction.

Thus to change $\frac{3}{4}$ to a decimal divide 4 into 3 and we get .75 as a result, thus:

$$4 \,\underline{|\, 3.00}$$
$$.75$$

In changing common fractions into decimals the former very often cannot be changed into the latter and not leave a remainder. But this fact does not at all prevent decimals from being used for all ordinary calculations, because in most examples the remainder is so slight it does not affect the general result.

In some cases the decimal may run up into the

tens and hundred thousandths; for instance take $\frac{4}{9}$ and change it into a decimal, then —

$$9 \,\underline{|\,4.0000000}$$
$$.4444444$$

From this it will be seen that the decimal will never be complete and so for all practical work it is usual to call it simply .44.

If the result is a decimal such as .8359 it is the common practice to call it .84 because the last figure, 9, is nearer 10 than it is to 1 and so we call it 10; and if we call it 10 then the next figure, which is 5, would be called a 6, thus .836. Now 6 is nearer 10 than it is to 1, so that calling the 6 a 10 the 3 becomes 4, hence we write .84, and this is close enough for all ordinary purposes.

Addition of Decimals. — The operation of adding decimals is exactly the same as that of adding whole numbers, thus:

```
. |735
. |720
. |012
. |467 or .47 (Answer)
```

Before starting to add put the decimal points down for the answer in the column of decimal points as shown above and then it will always be in the right place.

Subtraction of Decimals. — In the subtraction of decimals set the subtrahend and minuend down exactly as in the operation of subtracting whole numbers and place all the decimal points in a column as described above under the caption of *Addition of Decimals*, thus:

```
 2.821
  .960
 -----
 1.861 or 1.86 (Answer)
```

Multiplication of Decimals. — While the operation of multiplying decimals is exactly the same as that of multiplying whole numbers care must be taken to get the decimal point in the right place.

The rule for placing the decimal point in the product obtained by multiplying decimals is this:

Rule. — Add the number of decimal places in the multiplicand to those in the multiplier and, beginning at the right of the product, point off the sum obtained, thus:

```
   4.325 (Three places in the multiplicand) +
     .25 (Two places in the multiplier) =
 -------
  21625
  8650
 -------
 1.08125 (Five places in the product)
 (.54321)
```

Figuring Percentage by Decimals. — Figuring money percentages by means of decimals is short, quick, and easy for it is only necessary to multiply the per cent by the amount.

Per cent is always taken as hundredth parts of a dollar, for instance, instead of writing 5 per cent when we are doing a problem of this sort we simply write .05 or five one-hundredths ($\frac{5}{100}$)

Example: Suppose that you have a first mortgage of $97.00 on your new bungalow at 5 per cent per annum and you want to know how much you will owe at the end of the first year. Simply multiply $97.00 by 5, thus:

$$\begin{array}{r} \$97.00 \\ .05 \\ \hline \$4.8500 \end{array} \text{ or } \$4.85 \text{ (Answer)}$$

Point off four places, because there are two places in the multiplicand (00) and two places in the multiplier (05) pointed off and together these make four places.

Division of Decimals. — The division of decimals is perhaps a little harder than the foregoing operations; however there are very few examples in division, except those which come out even, which do not employ decimals.

To Divide a Whole Number into a Whole Number when there is a Remainder.

Rule A. — Divide as usual, except a decimal point should be placed after the last figure of the dividend and two or more ciphers must be annexed to it, according to the number of decimal places you want to have in the answer, thus:

Example: 143 ÷ 35 = 4.085 (Answer)

Now by annexing three ciphers, 143 with the

decimal point becomes 143.000, so we write the example like this:

```
      4.085 (Answer)
  35)143.000
     140
      300
      280
       200
```

It will be seen that the decimal point in the answer is placed directly above that in the dividend, the process of dividing being exactly the same as for ordinary division.

To Divide a Decimal into a Whole Number.

Rule B. — Annex as many ciphers to the dividend as there are decimal places in the divisor and this changes the problem into one like that described in Rule *A*, that is, one where a whole number is divided into a whole number thus:

Example: $625 \div .25 = 2500$

In this example 625 with two ciphers added becomes 62500 because there are two decimal places in the decimal .25. The example for this reason is written —

```
     2500. (Answer)
  25)62500.
     50
     125
     125
      00
```

Here the annexing of two ciphers to the dividend changes the decimal into a whole number. In other words we have multiplied both the divisor and the dividend by 100 by means of a short mental cut, thus:

$$625 \times 100 = 62500$$
$$.25 \times 100 = 25$$

So that we have changed the divisor which was a decimal into a whole number.

To Divide a Decimal by a Decimal.

Rule C. — To divide a decimal by a decimal start at the left of the decimal point of the dividend and point off as many places as there are places in the divisor, thus:

Example: 1.548 ÷ .36 = 4.3 (Answer)

Since there are two places in the divisor 1.548 becomes 154.8 and the operation is —

```
      4.3(Answer)
36)154.8
   144
    108
    108
```

To Change a Decimal into a Common Fraction. — Occasionally it is necessary to change a decimal into a common fraction, as for

Example: Change .725 into a common fraction.

Rule. — First write the decimal as if it were a whole number, that is without the decimal point.

Then draw the fraction line, count the number of decimal places in the decimal and set down an equal number of ciphers and prefix a 1, thus:

$$\frac{725}{1000}$$

Since there are three decimal places in the decimal, in the above example there must be three ciphers in the denominator or the lower part of the fraction.

CHAPTER VII

EXTRACTING SQUARE AND CUBE ROOTS

To figure out the square or cube root of a number is not an altogether simple operation, but if you set your work down systematically and follow the rules here given you will have no trouble.

SQUARE ROOT

To begin with we know that $1 = 1^2$, $100 = 10^2$, $10000 = 100^2$, etc., and this being true then the square root of any number between 1 and 100 must be some number between 1 and 10.

The above statement may be put in another form by saying that the square root of any two-figure number is a one-figure number, the square root of any three or four-figure number is a two-figure number, and so on.

Now if we have a large number which we want to find the square root of, say for example

$$4225$$

the first step is to divide it into two numbers of two figures each, thus:

2d pair	1st pair
42	25

where 25 may be considered as the first number pair and 42 as the second number pair and hence our answer must be a two-figure number.

To find the square root of a four-figure number such as our example calls for, work it out in the following manner:

	2d pair	1st pair	square root
	42	25	65 (Answer)
	36		
125	6	25	
	6	25	

First step. — Take the nearest square of the second pair, which in this case is the square of 6. Set the 6 down in the answer and set the square (36) down under the second pair, then subtract and bring down the first pair.

Second step. — Next multiply the 6 set down in the answer by 2; this gives 12 as the product and this (12) is called the *trial divisor*. Divide the 12 into the first two figures of the remainder (625), or in other words divide the 12 into the 62 and as it is easy to see that it will go 5 times set down 5 in the answer.

Third step. — Now annex a 5 to the 12, making 125, and multiply this number by the 5 in the answer. In this case there is no remainder and so the square root of 4225 is 65. (Answer)

To extract the square root of a larger number, say

43681

proceed as follows:

3d pair	2d pair	1st pair	square root
4	36	81	209 (Answer)
4			
409	36	81	
	36	81	

Solution. — Since 4 is the trial divisor and is not contained in 3, set down a cipher in the answer and annex another cipher to the 4, which makes the 4 a 40.

Then bring down the first number pair (81); using 40 as a trial divisor divide 40 into 368, this gives 9 as the quotient and hence annex 9 to the 40 and set down 9 in the answer also. The final step is to multiply 409 by the 9 in the answer.

When extracting the square root of a number which does not come out even, that is a number whose square root is a whole number and a decimal, proceed as usual but annex a pair of ciphers to the number and extract the square root to as many decimal places as you wish.

CUBE ROOT

To extract the cube root of a number is not a harder operation than finding the square root.

Since we know that $1 = 1^3$, $1{,}000 = 10^3$, and

$1{,}000{,}000 = 100^3$, etc., it must be clear that the cube root of any number between 1 and 1,000 must be some number which lies between 1 and 10; in a like manner the cube root of any number between 1,000 and 1,000,000 must be some number between 10 and 100.

Expressing this in another way we may say that the cube root of any three-figure number is a one-figure number while that of any five-figure number is a two-figure number and so forth.

If then we have a large number and we want to take its cube root the first step is to divide it into parts of three figures starting from the right; take for example:

91,125

divide it into parts of three figures, thus:

1st part	2d part
91	125

Now to find the cube root of 91,125 proceed as follows:

1st part	2d part	cube root
91	125	|45 (Answer)
64		
27		

Steps in the Solution

$$3 \times 40^2 = 4800$$
$$3 \times (40 \times 5) = 600$$
$$5^2 = 25$$
$$\text{Adding } 5425$$

First step. — Take the nearest cube of the first number part (91). In this case it is 64 and the cube root of 64 is 4 since $4 \times 4 \times 4 = 64$. Set this cube root (4) down in the answer and then subtract the 64 from the first part number (91).

Second step. — The remainder is 27,125 and in order to find a number that will go into 27,125 evenly (if the number you are taking the cube root of is a perfect cube) proceed as follows:

(*a*) Annex a cipher to the 4 in the answer, square it and multiply it by 3 thus:

$$40^2 \times 3 = 4800$$

(*b*) The first two figures of this product, that is, 48, is what is known as the trial divisor. Divide the first three figures of 27125 by 48, thus:

$$271 \div 48 = 5$$

(*c*) Next annex a cipher to the 4 in the answer, multiply it by the 5 just found, and then by 3 thus:

$$3 \times (40 \times 5) = 600$$

(*d*) Now square the 5 just found and add the three products together thus:

$$4800 + 600 + 25 = 5425$$

(*e*) This number, 5425, when multiplied by the 5 found by the trial divisor in part *b* should equal the remainder found in step *a*, that is $5425 \times 5 = 27125$.

(*f*) So that the 5 should now be set down in the answer and the cube root of 91,125 is 45.

Should the number not be a perfect cube and the root does not come out even then annex three ciphers to the number in parts of three, when the root may be carried out to as many decimal places as desired.

CHAPTER VIII

USEFUL TABLES AND FORMULAS

I. The Roman Numerals
II. Measure of Length
III. Other Measures of Length
IV. Measure of Area
V. Land Measure
VI. Measure of Volume
VII. Measure of Capacity (Liquid)
VIII. Apothecaries' Fluid Measure
IX. Dry Measure
X. Avoirdupois Weight
XI. Apothecaries' Weight
XII. Troy Weight

Weight by Carat
Fineness of Gold

Rule for Changing Parts by Volume to Parts by Weight

XIII. Comparison of Weights
XIV. Household Measure
XV. Miscellaneous Measure

Measures of Circles and Angles

XVI. Circular or Angular Measure by Degrees
XVII. Angular Measure by Radians
XVIII. Astronomical Measure
XIX. Geographical Measure
XX. Decimal Equivalents of Fractions of an Inch

Metric System of Weights and Measures

XXI. Measure of Length
XXII. Measure of Surface

XXIII. Measure of Land
XXIV. Measure of Volume (Cubic Measure)
XXV. Measure of Volume (Wood Measure)
XXVI. Measure of Volume (for Liquids and Solids)
XXVII. Measure of Weight

A Key to the Metric System

Rules for Measuring Surfaces and Solids

A — Triangle
B — Triangle
Parallelogram
Square or Rhombus
Trapezium
Circle
Ellipse

Rules for Measuring Circles and Spheres

Circumference of a Circle
Area of a Circle
Surface of a Sphere
Volume of a Sphere

Rules for Computing Simple Interest

Table I, The Roman Numerals

1 = I
2 = II
3 = III
4 = IV
5 = V
6 = VI
7 = VII
8 = VIII
9 = IX
10 = X
20 = XX
30 = XXX
40 = XL
50 = L
60 = LX
70 = LXX
80 = LXXX
90 = XC
100 = C

500 = D or LƆ
1,000 = M or CƆ
2,000 = MM or IIƆƆƆ
5,000 = $\overline{\text{V}}$ or LƆƆ
6,000 = $\overline{\text{VI}}$ or MMM
10,000 = $\overline{\text{X}}$ or CƆƆ
50,000 = $\overline{\text{L}}$ or LƆƆƆ
60,000 = $\overline{\text{LX}}$ or MMMƆ
100,000 = $\overline{\text{C}}$ or CƆƆƆ
1,000,000 = $\overline{\text{M}}$ or CƆƆƆƆ
2,000,000 = $\overline{\text{MM}}$ƆƆƆ

When a line is drawn over a number it means that its value is increased 1000 times.

English System of Weights and Measures

Table II, Measure of Length

12 inches	=	1 foot
3 feet	=	1 yard
$5\frac{1}{2}$ yards	=	1 rod
320 rods	=	1 statute mile

Table III, Other Measures of Length

1 size	=	$\frac{1}{3}$ inch (Used by shoemakers)
1 hand	=	4 inches (Used in measuring the height of horses)
1 fathom	=	6 feet (Used in measuring the depth of the sea)
1 chain	=	100 links = 22 yards (Used by surveyors)
1 furlong	=	40 rods = 220 yards
1 knot	=	$1.52\frac{2}{3}$ statute miles or 6,086 feet Used in measuring distances at sea)

Table IV, Measure of Area

144 square inches	=	1 square foot
9 square feet	=	1 square yard
$30\frac{1}{4}$ square yards	=	1 square rod
16 square rods	=	1 square chain
10 square chains	=	1 acre
160 square rods	=	1 acre
4840 square yards	=	1 acre
640 acres	=	1 square mile
100 square feet	=	1 square (Used in measuring roofing, flooring, etc.)

Table V, Land Measure

A township has 36 sections, each 1 mile square.

A section is 640 acres.

A quarter section $\frac{1}{2}$ mile square is 160 acres.

An eighth section $\frac{1}{2}$ mile long and $\frac{1}{4}$ mile wide is 80 acres.

Sections are all numbered from 1 to 36, commencing at the northeast corner.

One acre contains 4,840 square yards, or 43,560 square feet.

A lot $208\frac{2}{3}$ feet square contains 1 acre.

Table VI, Measure of Volume

1728 cubic inches	= 1 cubic foot
$24\frac{3}{4}$ cubic feet	= 1 perch
27 cubic feet	= 1 cubic yard
128 cubic feet	= 1 cord (Used in measuring wood, etc.)
1 cubic yard	= 1 load (Used in measuring earth, etc.)

Table VII, Measure of Capacity—Liquid

4 gills	= 1 pint
2 pints	= 1 quart
4 quarts	= 1 gallon
1 gallon	= 4 quarts = 8 pints = 32 gills
$31\frac{1}{2}$ gallons	= 1 barrel
63 gallons	= 1 hogshead

Table VIII, Apothecaries' Fluid Measure

60 minims	=	1 fluid drachm (f ʒ)
8 fluid drachms	=	1 fluid ounce (f ℥)
16 fluid ounces	=	1 pint (O)
8 pints	=	1 gallon (Cong.)

Table IX, Dry Measure

2 pints	=	1 quart
8 quarts	=	1 peck
4 pecks	=	1 bushel

Measures of Weight

Weight is the measure of the attraction between the earth and bodies upon or near its surface. There are four kinds of weight used in the United States and these are (*a*) *avoirdupois*, (*b*) *apothecaries'*, (*c*) *troy*, and (*d*) *metric*.

(*a*) Avoirdupois is the kind of weight that is used for all ordinary commercial purposes such as weighing sugar and other staple articles.

(*b*) Apothecaries' weight is the kind used by druggists in compounding prescriptions; but druggists buy their drugs and chemicals by avoirdupois weight.

(*c*) Troy weight is used by goldsmiths and jewellers and also by the U.S. Mint for weighing coins.

(*d*) Metric weight is used for nearly all scientific measurement. It will be fully described under the caption of Metric Weights and Measures.

Table X, Avoirdupois Weight

16 ounces	= 1 pound
100 pounds	= 1 hundred-weight
20 hundred-weight	= 1 ton = 2000 pounds

A *short* ton is 2000 pounds.

A *long* ton is 2240 pounds (also called a gross ton).

A *metric* ton is 2204.6 pounds. (See metric system).

Table XI, Apothecaries' Weight

20 grains	= 1 scruple
3 scruples	= 1 dram
8 drams	= 1 ounce
12 ounces	= 1 pound

Table XII, Troy Weight

24 grains	= 1 pennyweight
20 pennyweights	= 1 ounce
12 ounces	= 1 pound

Weight by Carat

A *carat*, or as it is sometimes written, *karat*, is the unit used for weighing precious stones. The international carat is equal to 3.168 grains, or 205 milligrams.

Fineness of Gold

The word *carat*, or *karat*, is also used to indicate the proportion of gold in a gold alloy. The carat is the 24th part by weight of a gold alloy and is derived from a weight equal to the $\frac{1}{24}$ part of a *gold mark* which was a unit of weight used in many European countries before the metric system was adopted. This gold which is said to be 18 carats fine is an alloy containing $\frac{18}{24}$ or $\frac{3}{4}$ parts of pure gold, the other $\frac{6}{24}$ being some inferior metal.

Table XIII, Comparison of Weights

Kind	*Pound*	*Ounce*	*Grain*
Avoirdupois	7000 gr.	$437\frac{1}{2}$ gr.	1
Apothecaries'	5760 gr.	480 gr.	1
Troy	5760 gr.	480 gr.	1

Table XIV, Household Measure

120 drops of water	= 1 teaspoonful
60 drops of thick liquid	= 1 teaspoonful
1 teaspoonful of thick liquid	= 1 ounce
2 teaspoonsful	= 1 dessert-spoonful
3 teaspoonsful	= 1 tablespoonful
16 tablespoonsful	= 1 cup
1 cup	= $\frac{1}{2}$ pint
1 cup of water	= $\frac{1}{2}$ pound

Rule for Changing Parts by Volume or Measure to Parts by Weight

The different substances which are used for recipes are sometimes given by volume or measure and sometimes by weight. It is often convenient to change the parts by volume into parts by weight and this can be done by multiplying the parts by volume by the *density*, that is, the *specific gravity*, of the substance which it is desired to change and the product obtained will be the parts by weight.

Table XV, Miscellaneous Measure

12 articles	= 1 dozen
12 dozen	= 1 gross
24 sheets of paper	= 1 quire
20 quires	= 1 ream
2 reams	= 1 bundle
5 bundles	= 1 bale

Measure of Circles and Angles

Since circles are of varying diameters they are measured by unit spaces called *degrees*. A degree (°) is the 360th part of a circle. Each degree is further divided into minutes (′) and the minutes into seconds (″), as the following table shows.

Angles are also measured by degrees; a right angle or quadrant is 90° and hence there are four right angles or quadrants in a circle.

Table XVI, Circular of Angular Measure by Degrees

60 seconds	= 1 minute
60 minutes	= 1 degree
90 degrees	= 1 quadrant or right angle
360 degrees	= 1 circle

Angular Measure by Radians

Another way to measure an angle is by its *radian.* A radian is the arc of a circle whose length is equal to the radius of the circle of which it is a part. The kind of angles most often used are right angles and angles less than 90°.

Table XVII

1 minute	=	60 seconds
1 degree	=	60 minutes
90 degrees	=	1 right angle
1 radian	=	$180 \div \pi = 57° 17' 45''$
1 degree	=	$\pi \div 180 = 0.017453$ radian

Note — For the value of π (Greek letter pi) see Table.

Table XVIII, Astronomical Measure

Sometimes astronomers use the following divisions of the circle:

12 signs	of 30	degrees	each	= 1 circle
6 sextants	of 60	"	"	= 1 circle
4 quadrants	of 90	"	"	= 1 circle

Table XIX, Geographical Measure

1 geographical mile	=	6087.15 feet
1 geographical mile	=	1.15287 statute mile
60 geographical miles	=	1 degree of longitude at the equator
360 degrees	=	the circumference of the earth at the equator

Table XX, Decimal Equivalents of Fractions of an Inch

8ths	16ths	32ds	64ths	Decimal Equivalents	8ths	16ths	32ds	64ths	Decimal Equivalents
			1	.015625				33	.515625
		1		.03125			17		.53125
			3	.046875				35	.546875
	1			.0625		9			.5625
			5	.078125				37	.578125
		3		.09375			19		.59357
			7	.109375				39	.609375
1				.125	5				.625
			9	.140625				41	.640625
		5		.15625			21		.65625
			11	.171875				43	.671875
	3			.1875		11			.6875
			13	.203125				45	.703125
		7		.21875			23		.71875
			15	.234375				47	.734375
2(¼″)				.25	6(¾″)				.75
			17	.265625				49	.765625
		9		.28125			25		.78125
			19	.296875				51	.796875
	5			.3125		13			.8125
			21	.328125				53	.828125
		11		.34375			27		.84375
			23	.359375				55	.859375
3				.375	7				.875
			25	.390625				57	.890625
		13		.40625			29		.90625
			27	.421875				59	.921875
	7			.4375		15			.9375
			29	.453125				61	.953125
		15		.46875			31		.96875
			31	.484375				63	.984375
4(½″)				.5	8(1″)				1.0

Metric System of Weights aud Measures

The metric system of weights and measures is like the Arabic system of notation and the United States money system in that it is based on the decimal system; that is, its divisions and multiples are all in the ratio of 10.

The metric unit of length is the *meter* and all other weights and measures of the metric system are based on the meter. The meter is the one ten-millionth part of the distance of the equator from the pole. Its length is equivalent to 39.37 inches.

The names of the different weights and measures express their value, the Latin prefixes indicate the fractional parts of the meter and the Greek prefixes indicating multiples larger than the meter. These prefixes are:

Table XXI, Measure of Length
(Common Table)

10 millimeters =	**1 centimeter** =	0.001	meter
10 centimeters =	1 decimeter =	0.01	"
10 decimeters =	**1 meter** =	0.1	"
10 meters =	1 decameter =	1	"
10 decameters =	1 hectometer =	10	meters
10 hectometers =	**1 kilometer** =	100	"
10 kilometers =	1 myriameter=	1,000	"
10 myriameters=		10,000	"

The denominations set in blackfaced type are those in common use.

Table XXII, Measure of Surface

100	square	millimeters	= 1	square	centimeter
100	"	centimeters	= 1	"	decimeter
100	"	decimeters	= 1	"	meter
100	"	meters	= 1	"	decameter
100	"	decameters	= 1	"	hectometers
100	"	hectometers	= 1	"	kilometer

Table XXIII, Measure of Land

The unit of area is the *are* and it is equal to one square decameter.

1 are	=	1000 milliares, ma
1 "	=	100 centiares, ca
1 "	=	10 deciares, da
10 ares	=	1 dekare, Da
100 "	=	1 hectare, Ha

Table XXIV, Measure of Volume

(Cubic Measure)

The unit of volume is the *cubic meter.*

1000 cubic millimeters	=	1 cubic centimeter
100 cubic centimeters	=	1 cubic decimeter
1000 cubic decimeter	=	1 cubic meter

Table XXV, Measure of Volume

(Wood Measure)

In measuring wood, excavations, and the like a unit called the *stere* is used and equals one cubic meter.

1 stere, s	=	100 centisteres, cs
1 "	=	10 decisteres, ds
10 steres	=	1 decastere, Ds
100 "	=	1 hectostere, Hs
1000 "	=	1 kilostere, Ks

Table XXVI, Measure of Volume

(For Liquids and Solids)

The *liter* is the unit of capacity and is equal to one cubic decimeter.

10 milliters, ml	=	1 centiliter cl
10 centiliters	=	1 deciliters, dl
10 deciliters	=	1 liter, l
10 liters	=	1 decaliter, Dl
10 decaliters	=	1 hectoliter, Hl
10 hectoliters	=	1 kiloliter, Kl

Table XXVII, Measure of Weight

10 milligrams, mg	=	1 centigram, cg
10 centigrams	=	1 decigram, dg
10 decigrams	=	1 gram, g
10 grams	=	1 decagram, Dg
10 decagrams	=	1 hectogram, Hg
10 hectograms	=	1 kilogram, Kg
10 kilograms	=	1 myriagram, Mg
10 myriagrams	=	1 quintal, Q
10 quintals	=	1 tonneau, T

A Key to the Metric System

In the nickel five-cent piece of U. S. coinage we have a key to the metric system of weights and measures. The diameter of this coin is 2 centimeters and its weight is 5 grams. Five of these coins placed in a row will, of course, have a length equal to 1 decimeter, and two of them will weigh a decagram.

As the kiloliter is a cubic meter, a key to the measure of length is also a key to the measure of capacity. If therefore you will carry a five-cent nickel for a pocket-piece you will always have a key to the entire metric system of weights and measures with you.

Rules for Measuring Surfaces and Solids

Parallelogram. — To find the area of a parallelogram, multiply its length, or *base* as it is called, by its height, or *altitude* as it is called, or expressed in the simple form of an algebraic equation. —

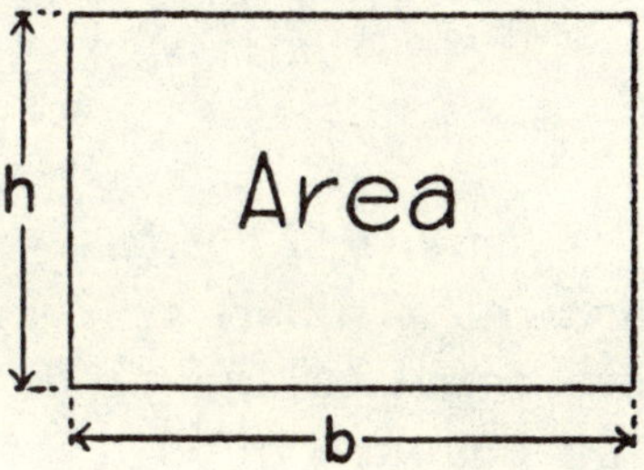

$$A = b \times h$$

Triangle. — To find the area of a triangle when the base and altitude are given, multiply its base by its altitude and divide by 2, or

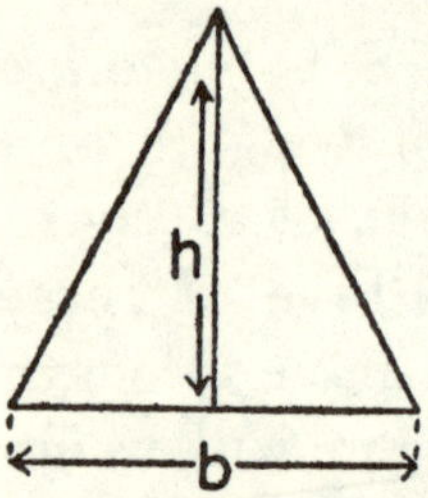

$$A = \frac{bh}{2}$$

Triangle. — To find the area when three sides are given take half the sum of the three sides, subtract each side separately from this sum; then multiply half the sum of the three sides of the three remainders, and, finally, take the square root of this product, thus:

First step $\frac{a + b + c}{2}$

Second step $\frac{a + b + c}{2} - a$

Third step $\frac{a + b + c}{2} - b$

Fourth step $\frac{a + b + c}{2} - c$

Square or Rhombus. — The area of a square or rhombus are equal to the product of the diagonals divided by 2, or

$$A = \frac{ab}{2}$$

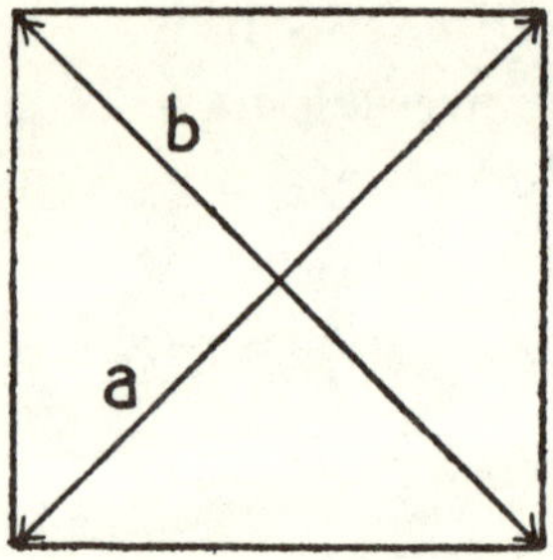

Trapezium.—The area of a trapezium is equal to half the product of the sum of the two parallel sides by the distance between them, or

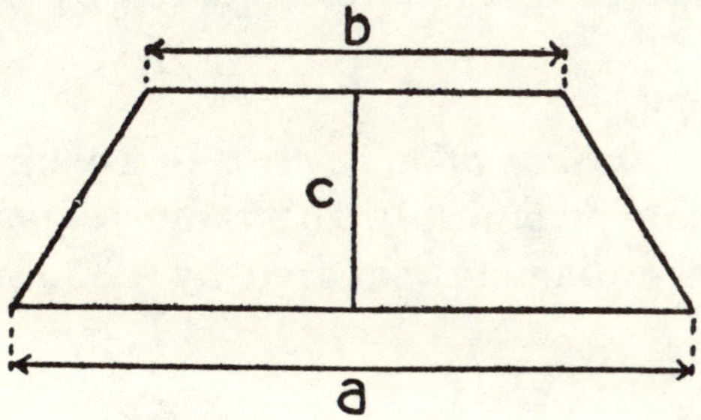

$$A = \frac{(a + b) \times c}{2}$$

Circle. — The area of a circle equals the square of the diameter times .7854, or

$$A = .7854 \times d^2$$

Ellipse. — The area of an ellipse equals the product of the long and short axes multiplied by .7854, or

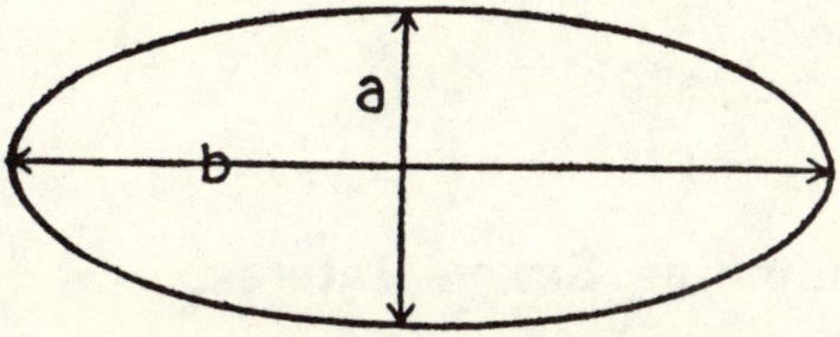

$$A = a \times b \times .7854$$

Rules for Measuring Circles and Spheres

Circumference of a Circle. — To find the circumference of a circle multiply its diameter by 3.1416 or expressed by a simple algebraic formula —

$$\pi D$$

Where π (Greek letter pi) = 3.1416 and
D = the diameter

Area of a Circle. — To find the area multiply the radius of the circle squared by 3.1416, or

$$\pi R^2$$

Surface of a Sphere. — To find the surface of a sphere multiply the radius squared, or 3.1416, by the diameter squared by 12.5664

or $$4\pi R^2$$
or $$\pi D^2$$

Volume of a Sphere. — To find the volume of a sphere multiply the radius of the circle cubed by

$$\frac{12.5664}{3}$$

or $$\frac{3.1416}{6} \times \text{the diameter cubed}$$
or $$\tfrac{4}{3}\pi R^3$$
or $$\tfrac{1}{6}\pi D^3$$

Rules for Computing Simple Interest

The following are simple rules for finding the interest on any principal for any number of days. When the principal contains cents, point off four places from the right of the result to express the interest in dollars and cents. When the principal contains dollars only point off two places.

2 per cent, multiply the principal by the number of days to run and divide by 180.

$2\frac{1}{2}$ per cent, multiply by number of days and divide by 144.

3 per cent, multiply by number of days and divide by 120.

$3\frac{1}{2}$ per cent, multiply by number of days and divide by 102.86.

4 per cent, multiply by number of days and divide by 90.

5 per cent, multiply by number of days and divide by 72.

6 per cent, multiply by number of days and divide by 60.

7 per cent, multiply by number of days and divide by 51.43.

8 per cent, multiply by number of days and divide by 45.

9 per cent, multiply by number of days and divide by 40.

10 per cent, multiply by number of days and divide by 36.

12 per cent, multiply by number of days and divide by 30.

15 per cent, multiply by number of days and divide by 24.

18 per cent, multiply by number of days and divide by 20.

20 per cent, multiply by number of days and divide by 18.

CHAPTER IX

MAGIC WITH FIGURES

The Magic Squares
Second Sight with Dice
Telling a Person's Age
Thirteen Six Times in Twelve
How Figures Lie
1001 Different Deals with 13 Cards
Napier's Rods — A Mechanical Short Cut to Multplication and Division
Puzzle — Watchful Waiting
How to Become a Lightning Calculator in Ten Seconds

Magic Squares. — The magic square is an arrangement of numbers in the cells of a square in such a fashion that however the rows are added, whether vertically, horizontally, or diagonally, the sum in every case will be the same.

Thus in the magic square here shown the num-

1	16	11	6
13	4	7	10
8	9	14	3
12	5	2	15

bers from 1 to 16 are so disposed that whatever

row is added the sum is 34. There are over 800 different arrangements of possible number combinations for forming magic squares and no two will be alike.

Rules of various kinds have been worked out for constructing magic squares but no single rule has yet been found that is equally applicable for all of them.

Magic circles which consist of a number of concentric circles, that is circles within circles, can be formed by dividing their radii and numbering their sections after the manner of the magic squares, and when the numbers in each circle and row are added the sum will be the same *Magic cubes* and *magic cylinders* can also be constructed on the same principle.

For a fuller account of Magic Squares see *The Monist* 1906–07, Vol. XVI, page 56. Open Court Pub. Co., Chicago.

Also the *Occult Review*, Vol. III, 1906. Published by William Rider and Son Ltd., London. J. M. C. Hampson, 669 Sedgwick St., Chicago, Agent.

Second Sight With Dice

The Effect. — A pair o' dice are handed to some one with the request that he throw them while you turn your back or close your eyes or both so that you cannot see the numbers.

Next ask him to take a number on either die and to multiply it by 2, then add 5 and multiply the sum obtained by 5 and to this add the number on the other die and have him tell you the number he obtains from these operations.

From the number he gives you, you mentally subtract 25 and you will get two figures for the remainder, and these will be the two numbers on the dice.

Example: Suppose the number given you is 59; then 59 − 25 = 34, that is, the number on one die is 3 and the number on the other die is 4. The whole operation is as follows:

$3 \times 2 = 6 + 5 = 11 \times 5 = 55 + 4 = 59 - 25 = 34$

Telling a Person's Age

The Effect. — Ask a spectator to tell you in what columns of figures his or her age appears in the following table, when you will instantly tell his or her age.

The Rule. — By using the following table you need only to know what columns his age appears in and then add the top numbers of these columns together, when the sum will be the age of the person required.

Example: Suppose a person says that his age is given in columns A, C, and E, then —

$$1 + 4 + 16 = 21$$

hence the age value must be 21.

The numbers of bank-notes, dates of coins, the combinations of safes, the numbers of watches, the

TABLE

A	B	C	D	E	F
1	2	4	8	16	32
3	3	5	9	17	33
5	6	6	10	18	34
7	7	7	11	19	35
9	10	12	12	20	36
11	11	13	13	21	37
13	14	14	14	22	38
15	15	15	15	23	39
17	18	20	24	24	40
19	19	21	25	25	41
21	22	22	26	26	42
23	23	23	27	27	43
25	26	28	28	28	44
27	27	29	29	29	45
29	30	30	30	30	46
31	31	31	31	31	47
33	34	36	40	48	48
35	35	37	41	49	49
37	38	38	42	50	50
39	39	39	43	51	51
41	42	44	44	52	52
43	43	45	45	53	53
45	46	46	46	54	54
47	47	47	47	55	55
49	50	52	56	56	56
51	51	53	57	57	57
53	54	54	58	58	58
55	55	55	59	59	59
57	58	60	60	60	60
59	59	61	61	61	61
61	62	62	62	62	62
63	63	63	63	63	63

time one gets up in the morning or any other numbers thought of within the limits of the table may be told by this method with equal facility.

Thirteen Six Times in Twelve

To perform this curious operation in figures write down the following numbers:

1, 2, 3, 4, 5, 6, 7, 8, 9, 10, 11, 12

Now by adding the first and last numbers together you will have—

$$1 + 12 = 13$$
$$2 + 11 = 13$$
$$3 + 10 = 13$$
$$4 + 9 = 13$$
$$5 + 8 = 13$$
$$6 + 7 = 13$$

Thus with twelve numbers you get 13 six times.

How Figures Lie

A young fellow had worked for a grocer for seven years and got married, when it behooved him to ask the boss for a raise; so the latter (who was the original inventor of the wooden nutmeg) began to do a little figuring.

"You see," he pointed out to his clerk, "there are 365 days in a year and you work 8 hours a day, which makes $121\frac{1}{2}$ days; then there are 52 Sundays and subtracting these leaves $69\frac{1}{2}$ days. There are

13 legal 2 race, and 1 circus days, and taking these away $54\frac{1}{2}$ days are left.

"You have 1 hour for lunch every day which, summed up, makes 14 days and this leaves $40\frac{1}{2}$ days. Every Saturday afternoon you get off to bury your grandmother or help a maiden aunt hang pictures and this makes $25\frac{1}{2}$ days and leaves 14 days. Then I have to give you a vacation of two weeks every summer and this takes up the other 14 days. As the store is losing money I can't give you the raise anyway. Good-night."

1001 Different Deals with 13 Cards. — To ascertain how many different deals can be made by using 13 cards out of an ordinary pack proceed as follows:

First multiply the following terms: $52 \times 51 \times 50 \times 49 \times 48 \times 47 \times 46 \times 45 \times 44 \times 43 \times 42 \times 41 \times 40$. You will note that there are 13 terms in this multiplication.

Next multiply the following 13 terms: $13 \times 12 \times 11 \times 10 \times 9 \times 8 \times 7 \times 6 \times 5 \times 4 \times 3 \times 2 \times 1$; now divide the product of the first multiplication by the product of the second multiplication and the quotient will be the number of different deals that can be made with 13 out of a pack of 52 cards. If you know how to use *logarithms* you can short-cut the process very considerably.

Napier's Rods. — A wonderful short-cut device for multiplying and dividing was worked out three centuries ago by Lord Napier. It has not been very widely used since then in virtue of the fact that *logarithms*, which he also invented, have taken its place. It is however a very clever scheme and one that you can make use of to good advantage especially for the multiplication of large numbers.

A

1	1	2	3	4	5	6	7	8	9	0
2	2	4	6	8	1/0	1/2	1/4	1/6	1/8	0
3	3	6	9	1/2	1/5	1/8	2/1	2/4	2/7	0
4	4	8	1/2	1/6	2/0	2/4	2/8	3/2	3/6	0
5	5	1/0	1/5	2/0	2/5	3/0	3/5	4/0	4/5	0
6	6	1/2	1/8	1/4	3/0	3/6	4/2	4/8	5/4	0
7	7	1/4	2/1	2/8	3/5	4/2	4/9	5/6	6/3	0
8	8	1/6	2/4	3/2	4/0	4/8	5/6	6/4	7/2	0
9	9	1/8	2/7	3/6	4/5	5/4	6/3	7/2	8/1	0

A

Napier's Rods for Performing Multiplication Operations.

It consists of a set of ten rods having a square cross-section and an index-rod AA as shown in Fig. 1. This index-rod should be made stationary and it can be fastened to a board. The other ten rods should be loose so that they can be changed about.

A very serviceable set of rods can be made of strips of heavy cardboard $\frac{3}{8}$ inch wide and $3\frac{3}{4}$ inches long. These strips should then be divided off into squares with the figures marked in them in good black ink. Fig. 1 shows the set of rods or strips complete.

Now suppose that you want to multiply 3795

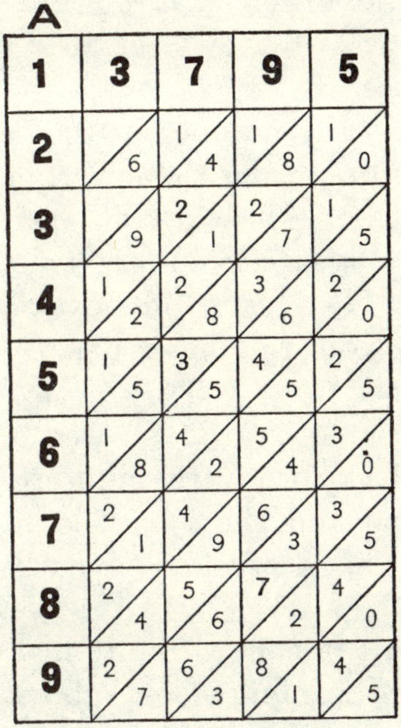

Rods Set to Multiply 3795 by 9.

by 9; the first thing to do is to move the rods having the numbers 3, 7, 9, and 5 at the top into the position shown in Fig. 2, and up against the index-rod AA. This done you are ready to perform the operation, thus:

Follow the last figure of the multiplicand, namely 5, down until you are opposite the 9 on the index-rod which you will see in the lower half of the square at 5 and set this figure down in your answer. Then add the 4 and the 1, that is, the number in the upper part of the square to the number in the lower part of the next square, and since 4 and 1 are 5 set this down in your answer.

Adding, now, the number in the top of the next square to the number in the lower part of the next square, that is, $8 + 3$, you will have 11, and set down the unit figure (1) in the answer and carry the tens figure (1) over to the next addition. Adding as before you will have $6 + 7 = 13$ plus the 1 carried equals 14.

Set down the 4 in the answer and carry the 1, and since the figure in the upper part of the last square is 2 you add the 1 carried to the 2 which makes 3; set this down and you will get for your answer 34155.

Sets of numbers can be multiplied just as easily as the simple example given above, for all you have to do is to slide the rods or strips on which the figures of the multiplicand are marked next to the index-rod.

Napier also devised a division table and you can make one by means of a table of the product of the divisor multiplied by each of the numbers from 1 to 9.

Puzzle — Watchful Waiting. — *The Question.*— At what points on the dial of a watch or clock will the hour and minute hands be in conjunction during 12 succeeding hours if they are started at exactly 12 o'clock?

The Answer. — At the following times during one complete revolution of the hour hand:

At	$5\frac{1}{2}$	minutes after	1
	11	" "	2
	$16\frac{1}{2}$	" "	3
	22	" "	4
	$27\frac{1}{2}$	" "	5
	33	" "	6
	38	" "	7
	$43\frac{1}{2}$	" "	8
	49	" "	9
	$54\frac{1}{2}$	" "	10
	60	" "	11

How to Become a Lightning Calculator in Ten Seconds. — This is a pretty trick with figures that has been used by many a lightning calculator (?) as a preliminary to the further exploit of distributing Yellowstone Kit's two dollar liver-pad for the small sum of one dollar.

The Effect. — You ask a spectator to write down a row of figures and then you write down a row; have him write another row and you write one under it; he writes a third row and you your third row, and so on without regard to the number of figures in the row or to the length of the column. Then you write down the sum as fast as you can chalk the figures on the board.

An Example:

First	row	65421
Second	"	34579
Third	"	52578
Fourth	"	47422
Fifth	"	97351
Sixth	"	2649
Seventh	"	23451
Eighth	"	12345
		335796

The Cause. — You will observe by referring to the above example that the corresponding figures of the first and second rows make 9 when added together, except the right hand ending figures which when added makes 10, thus:

6	5	4	2	1
3	4	5	7	9
9,	9,	9,	9,	10

And this also holds good for the third and fourth rows and for the fifth and sixth rows. The seventh and eighth rows however can be written either by the spectator or by yourself, and *any figures* may be used as long as they are *less* than 9.

To add the column start at the left and set down 3, since there are three sets of rows which you have artfully *doped out.* Then simply add the last two rows, setting down the figures in their proper order, thus:

	2	3	4	5	1
	1	2	3	4	5
3	3	5	7	9	6

and this is the answer.

Of course there is no real adding and the last two rows can be written anywhere in the example as long as the rows forming the couplets add to 9 with the two last figures adding to 10.

INDEX

INDEX

A

Adding backward, 25
Addition and subtraction combined, 31
Addition, bookkeeper's check, 24
Addition, cumulative, 7
Addition of decimals, 68
Addition, left-handed, two number, 22
Addition, lightning, 27
Addition, operation of, 25
Addition, period, 25
Addition, quick single column, 19
Addition, rapid, 16
Addition, simultaneous double column, 19
Addition, simultaneous three column, 23
Addition table, 16
Addition, three line exercise, 18
Addition, to check, 26
Age, telling a person's, 100
Algebra defined, 12
Algebraic formulas, 95
Aliquot parts, 64
Angles, measure of, 87
Angular measure by degrees, 87
Angular measure by radians, 88
Apothecaries' fluid measure, English, 84
Apothecaries' weight, English, 85
Arabic numerals, 3
Area, 93
Area, English measure of, 82
Area of circle, to find, 95
Area of ellipse, to find, 95
Area of parallelogram, to find, 93
Area of rhombus, to find, 94
Area of square to find, 94
Area of trapezium, to find, 95
Area of triangle, to find, 94
Arithmetic, definition of, 1
Arithmetical signs and symbols, 4
Arithmometer, 16
Astronomical measure, 88
Austrian method of subtraction, 30
Avoirdupois weight, English, 85

B

Bookkeeper's check addition, 24

C

Capacity, English measure of liquid, 83
Carat, weight by, 85
Cards, 1001 different deals with 13, 103
Centimeter, 90
Check addition, bookkeeper's, 24
Check addition, to, 26
Checking division by casting out Nines, 61
Checking division by the lightning method, 62
Checking multiplication by casting out nines, 53
Checking multiplication by division, 53

Checking multiplication by the lightning method, 54
Checking multiplication work, 53
Checking subtraction, 33
Circle, to find area of, 95
Circle, to find the circumference by algebra, 95
Circles, measure of, 87
Circles, rules for measuring, 95
Circular measure, by degrees, 87
Circumference of a circle by algebra, to find the, 95
Combined addition and subtraction, 31
Common fractions, 10
Comparison of English weights, 86
Complement method of multiplying, 50
Complement in subtraction, 28
Complex fractions, 10
Compound fractions, 10
Compound interest, 14
Continued fractions, 10
Counting, origin of, 3
Cross-multiplying, 14
Cube root, extracting, 76
Cubic measure, of volume, metric, 91
Cumulative addition, 7

D

Decimal equivalents of fractions of an inch, 89
Decimal fractions, 10
Decimal point, 11
Decimal system, 11
Decimal, to change a common fraction into a, 67
Decimals, 11 and 67
Decimals, addition of, 68
Decimals, division of, 70
Decimals, figuring percentage by, 69
Decimals, multiplication of, 69
Decimals, to change a decimal into a common fraction, 72
Decimals, to divide a decimal into a decimal, 72
Decimals, to divide a decimal into a whole number, 71
Decimals, to divide a whole number into a whole number when there is a remainder, 70
Decreased varying scales, 15
Definition of arithmetic, 1
Digits, meaning of, 3
Dividend, 9
Dividing a number by 25, or a multiple of 25, 59
Dividing any number by 10, 100, 1000, etc., 58
Dividing any number by a number joined by factors, 59
Dividing any number by a number formed of three factors, 60
Dividing any number by a number formed of factors; where there are no remainders, 60
Dividing any number by a number formed of factors; where there is a remainder, 60
Division, checking by casting out nines, 61
Division, checking by the lightning method, 62
Division, long, 9
Division of decimals, 70

Division of decimals, to divide a whole number into a whole number when there is no remainder, 70
Division, operation of, 9
Division, short cuts in, 56
Division sign, 5
Division, to divide a decimal by a decimal, 72
Division, to divide a decimal into a whole number, 71
Division, to divide a number by 25 or a Multiple of 25, 59
Division, to divide any number by 10, 100, 1000, etc., 58
Division, to divide any number by a number formed by three factors, 60
Division, to divide any number by a number formed by factors; where there are no remainders, 59
Division, to divide any number by a number formed by factors; where there is a remainder, 60
Division, to instantly find the division of a number, 56
Divisor, 9
Dry measure, English, 84

E

Ellipse, to find area of, 95
English system, of weights and measures, 82
Enumeration, origin of, 3
Equal sign, 4
Equivalent fractions of an inch, decimal, 89
Equivalent parts, 65
Evolution, 12
Extraction of roots, 12
Extracting square and cube root, 74

F

Factor in Powers, 12
Factors, 9
Figures, how they lie, 102
Figures, magic with, 98
Figures, origin of, 3
Finding the product of two numbers when both end in 5 and the tens are even, 38
Finding the product of two numbers when both end in 5 and the tens figures are uneven, 38
Finding the square of two numbers when both end in 5, 37
Fineness of gold, 85
Fluid measure, apothecaries', English, 84
Foot-pound-second system, 3
Formulas, algebraic, 95
Formulas, useful, 80
Fraction, to change a common fraction into a decimal, 67
Fraction, to change a decimal into a common fraction, 72
Fractions, 9
Fractions, common, 10
Fractions, complex, 10
Fractions, continued, 10
Fractions, decimal, 10
Fractions, improper, 10
Fractions of an inch, decimal equivalents of, 89
Fractions, proper, 10
Fractions, simple, 10

Fractions, vulgar, 10
Fundamental operations, 4

G

Geographical measure, 88
Gold, fineness of, 85
Gram, 92
Gross profit, 15
Ground rules, 4 and 5

H

Household measure, English, 86
How figures lie, 102

I

Improper fractions, 10
Increased varying scales, 15
Index in powers, 12
Instantly finding the divisor of a number, 56
Integers, 3
Interest, 14
Interest, compound, 14
Interest, rules for computing simple, 96
Interest, simple, 14
Involution, 11

K

Karat, see Carat, 85
Key to the twelve systems, 93
Kilogram, 92
Kilometer, 90

L

Land measure, English, 83
Land, metric measure of, 91
Left-handed two number addition, 22
Length, English measure of, 82
Length, metric measure of, 90
Lightning addition, 27
Lightning calculator, how to become one in 10 seconds, 107
Lightning method of checking division, 62
Lightning method of checking multiplication, 54
Liquid measure of capacity, English, 83
Liquids, metric measure by volume, 92
Liter, 92
Logarithms, 104
Loss, 14 and 15

M

Magic circles, 99
Magic cubes, 99
Magic cylinders, 99
Magic figures, 98
Magic squares, 98
Making change, method of subtraction, 30
Making-up method of subtraction, 30
Measure, apothecaries' fluid, English, 84
Measure, astronomical, 88
Measure, English dry, 84
Measure, English land, 83
Measure, geographical, 88
Measure, household, 86
Measure, miscellaneous, 87
Measurement, divisions of, 2
Measurement of time, length, and mass, 3
Measure of angles and circles, 87

Measure of angles by radius, 88
Measure of area, 82
Measure of land, metric, 90 and 91
Measure of length, English, 82
Measure of length, metric, 90
Measure of liquid capacity, English, 83
Measure of liquids by metric volume, 92
Measure of solids by metric volume, 92
Measure of surface, metric, 91
Measure of volume, cubic, metric, 91
Measure of volume, English, 83
Measure of volume, metric, 91
Measure of weight, English, 84
Measure of weight, metric, 92
Measure of wood by metric volume, 91
Measure, rule of changing parts by measure to parts by weight, 86
Measures, metric system of, 90
Measuring circles and spheres, rules for, 95
Measuring surfaces and solids, rule for, 93
Metric measure of land, 91
Metric measure of length, 90
Metric measure of liquids by volume, 92
Metric measure of solids by volume, 92
Metric measure of surface, 91
Metric measure of volume, 91
Metric measure of weight, 92
Metric system, 11
Metric system, a key to the, 93
Metric system of weights and measures, 90
Metric wood measure by volume, 91
Millimeter, 90
Minuend, 28
Minus sign, 4
Miscellaneous measure, 87
Multiplication, 47
Multiplication, lightning method of checking, 54
Multiplication of decimals, 69
Multiplication, operation of, 7
Multiplication, short cuts in, 35
Multiplication sign, 5
Multiplication table, 8 and 36
Multiplication table, a further extension of the, 37
Multiplication, to check by casting out nines, 53
Multiplication, to check by division, 53
Multiplication, to check the work, 53
Multiplication, to find the product of numbers when both end in 5 and the tens figures are even, 38
Multiplication, to find the product of two numbers when both end in 5 and the tens figures are uneven, 38
Multiplication, to find the square of two numbers when both end in 5, 37
Multiplication, to multiply a number by 21, 31, 41, etc., 43
Multiplication, to multiply a

number by 11, or any multiple of 11, 42
Multiplication, to multiply any number by 25 or 75, 40
Multiplication, to multiply a number by 101, 301, 501, etc., 44
Multiplication, to multiply any number by 10, 100, 1000, etc., 39
Multiplication, to multiply any number ending in ciphers by a multiple of 10, 40
Multiplication, to multiply any number by higher multiples of 25, 41
Multiplication, to multiply any number by a multiple of 10, 39
Multiplication, to multiply any number by a number formed of factors, 48
Multiplication, to multiply any two numbers of two figures each where the tens are alike, 48
Multiplication, to multiply any two numbers of two figures each where the units are alike, 47
Multiplication, to square a number having two figures, 45
Multiplying a number by 11 or any multiple of 11, 42
Multiplying a number by 21, 31, 41, etc., 43
Multiplying a number by 101, 301, 501, etc., 44
Multiplying any number by 25 or 75, 40
Multiplying any number by 10, 100, 1000, etc., 39
Multiplying any number ending in ciphers by a multiple of 10, 40
Multiplying any number by higher multiples of 25, 41
Multiplying any number by a multiple of 10, 39
Multiplying any number by a number formed of factors, 48
Multiplying any two numbers of two figures each where the tens are alike, 48
Multiplying any two numbers of two figures each where the units are alike, 47
Multiplying by the complement method, 50
Multiplying by the sliding method, 51
Multiplying by the supplement method, 50
Multiplying by the tens, 37
Multiplying, Cross-, 14

N

Napier's rods, 103
Net profit, 15
Number in powers, 12
Numerals, Roman, 81

O

Operation of addition, 2–5
Operation of division, 9
Operation of multiplication, 7
Operation of subtraction, 2–6
Origin of addition, 2
Origin of calculation, 1
Origin of counting, 3
Origin of figures, 3
Origin of fractions, 2
Origin of subtraction, 2

P

Parallelogram, to find area of, 93
Percentage, 14
Percentage by decimals, figuring, 69
Per centum, 14
Period addition, 25
Plus sign, 4
Powers, 11
Powers and roots, 11
Prehistoric man, 6
Primitive man, 2
Profit and loss, 14
Profit, gross, 15
Profit, net, 15
Proper fractions, 10
Proportion, 13
Puzzle — watchful waiting, 106

Q

Quick single column addition, 19
Quintal, 92
Quotient, 9
Quotient in ratios, 13

R

Radians, angular measure by, 88
Radical sign, 12
Rapid addition, 16
Rapid subtraction, 28
Rate, 14
Ratio, 8–13
Reduction of weights and measures, 15
Rhombus, to find area of, 94
Roman numerals, 81
Roots, 12
Rule for changing parts by volume or measure to parts by weight, 86
Rules for computing simple interest, 96
Rules for measuring circles and spheres, 95
Rules for measuring surfaces and solids, 93

S

Second sight with dice, 99
Short cuts in division, 56
Short cuts in multiplication, 35
Signs, arithmetical, 4
Simple fractions, 10
Simple interest, 14
Simple interest, rules for computing, 96
Simultaneous double column addition, 19
Simultaneous three column addition, 23
Sliding method of multiplying, 51
Solids, metric measure by volume of, 92
Solids, rules for measuring, 93
Sphere by algebra, to find the surface of a, 96
Sphere by algebra, to find the volume of a, 96
Spheres, rules for measuring, 95
Square, to find area of, 94
Square root, extracting, 74
Squaring a number having two figures, 45
Subtracting two or more numbers from two or more other numbers, 32
Subtraction, Austrian method, 30
Subtraction by addition, 30
Subtraction, checking, 33

Subtraction, making change method, 30
Subtraction, making-up method, 30
Subtraction, operation of, 2
Subtraction, rapid, 28
Subtraction table, 29
Subtraction, taking-away method, 28
Subtrahend, 28
Supplement method of multiplying, 50
Surface, metric measure of, 91
Surface of a sphere by algebra, to find, 96
Surfaces, rules for measuring, 93
Symbols, arithmetical, 4

T

Tables and formulas, useful, 80
Taking-away method of subtraction, 28
Telling a person's age, 100
Thinking down in subtraction, 28
Thirteen six times in twelve, 102
Times sign, 5
Ton, English long, 85
Ton, English short, 85
Ton, metric, 85
Tonneau, 92
Trapezium, to find area of, 95
Triangle, to find area of, 94
Troy weight, English, 85

U

Useful tables and formulas, 80

V

Varying scales, decreased, 15
Varying scales, increased, 15
Volume, English measure of, 83
Volume, metric cubic measure of, 91
Volume, metric measure of, 91
Volume, metric measure of liquid by, 92
Volume, metric measure of solids by, 92
Volume, metric wood measure, 91
Volume of a sphere by algebra, to find the, 96
Volume, rule for changing parts by volume to parts by weight, 86
Vulgar fractions, 10

W

Weight, apothecaries' English, 85
Weight by carat, 85
Weight, English avoirdupois, 85
Weight, English measure of, 84
Weight, English Troy, 85
Weight, metric measure of, 92
Weight, rule for changing parts by volume or measure to parts by, 86
Weights and measures, English, 82
Weights and measures, reduction of, 15
Weights, comparison of English, 86
Weights, metric system of, 90
Whole number, 6
Wood measure, metric volume, 91

X

X in albegra, 13